Best of Boulder
Bouldering

by Bob Horan

CHOCKSTONE®

FALCONGUIDES®

GUILFORD, CONNECTICUT
HELENA, MONTANA
AN IMPRINT OF THE GLOBE PEQUOT PRESS

FALCONGUIDES®

Cover photo: Jay Droeger boulders up the *Original Line* while Peter Mortimer spots, Eden Rocks, Green Mountain West Ridge. Photo by Bob Horan.

Library of Congress Cataloging-in-Publication Data is available on file.

ISBN 978-1-58592-004-4

Printed in the United States of America
10 9 8 7 6 5 4 3 2

This book is dedicated to my children.

CONTENTS

MAP LEGEND

Interstate Highway		Interstate Highway	5
Paved Road (major)		U.S. Highway	2 395
Paved Road (minor)		State/County Roads	23 166
Fire Road		Forest Service Road	4420
Tunnel		Bridge	
Trail		Peak/Elevation	x
Railroad		Crag/Boulder	
Railroad Tunnel		Cliff	cliff face
Forest/Park Boundary		Talus	
Gate		Mine Site	
River/Creek		Pitch Number	28
Lake		Tree	
Buildling	■ or □		
Parking	P	Compass	N
Steps			
Tension Wire		Scale	0 1 2 Miles

BOULDER OVERVIEW

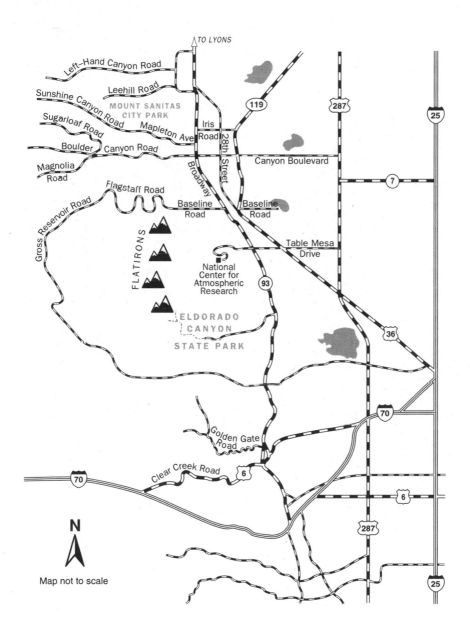

N

Map not to scale

INTRODUCTION

Bouldering is at the heart of all climbing. A boulderer utilizes gymnastic, acrobatic, and aerobatic techniques—the outcrops and boulders are the apparatus and each individual problem is a unique performance. Strength, dexterity, poise, grace, and balance are developed on the boulders. For the serious boulderer, difficulty and style are the equal goals. Endurance and recovery are also greatly enhanced through bouldering, and it is on the short cliffs that the all-important mental parameters of the sport are honed.

The Best of Boulder Bouldering is a compilation of the best boulders that the Boulder area has to offer. Much of this knowledge was gained from personal and shared experience over the last thirty years. Within this book you will find new bouldering areas being revealed for the first time. Seventy-five percent of this hard-earned knowledge has not been published.

The search for newer boulders in the Boulder area began with the realization that there was still a lot of virgin rock with the potential for new routes. Many fall lines on boulders flowing off the slopes were explored. This exploration soon transformed into a desire to check out every nook and cranny of rock for prime boulders within the magnificent Flatirons Range. Each new discovery served as soul food, feeding the fire of the quest. Traditionally, areas such as Eldorado Canyon and Flagstaff Mountain have been the hot spots for the area's bouldering enthusiasts, and for good reason. Actually, however, these rocks are but a small percentage of what the Flatirons truly have to offer. Hundreds of new virgin boulders exist throughout the range, and I developed criteria to help me select which new ones to work on. Many of the problems took several repeat visits over many months to complete. The following standards guided my quest:

- The boulder must have a reasonably safe landing zone (even so, pads and spotters are recommended for all problems).

- The boulder should have moderate to difficult problems.

- The problems on the boulder should qualify as classic. (All of the problems included in this book are thought to be classics).

This book will give you the information you need to access these natural treasures. The excellent rock quality and the beauty of these boulders and their surroundings is an experience I hope you will enjoy and help preserve for many generations to come. Residents as well as visitors to the Boulder area are fortunate to have one of the world's greatest concentrations of boulders to climb on and explore. Variations in rock type, holds, steepness, and environment provide bouldering and training possibilities for climbers of all abilities. Good climbing and enjoy!

ARRANGEMENT OF TEXT

The bouldering areas are described from north to south beginning with the boulders of Mount Sanitas, then proceeding south to Boulder Canyon, Flagstaff Mountain, and the Sacred Cliffs. Farther south, the descriptions continue with the Flatirons, beginning with the Bluebells (First, Second, and Third Flatirons), then farther south to Skunk Canyon, Bear Canyon, and Fern Canyon. This is followed by the boulders east of the Maiden and Matron, and then Shadow Canyon and Eldorado Canyon are described. The scope of this book ends far south with the boulders in the meadows east of Mickey Mouse Wall. Area maps and text describing the position of the boulders in relation to each of these canyons and their prominent formations are presented in an easy-to-use manner. Descriptive photos of all the boulders and problems accompany the text. Ninety-nine percent of the descriptive boulder photos have a climber on them for size scaling and perspective.

RATINGS

I decided to use the V system as the core rating system throughout the book, although a B rating will accompany some of the older classics (problems created before 1995). For problems that are highball (far off the ground), an (**hb**) will follow the rating. Those that are extremely dangerous and highball will be accompanied by an (**xhb**). On the (**hb**) problems a crash pad and spotter(s) are seriously recommended. On (**xhb**) problems a toprope is seriously recommended.

The V system rating has, without a doubt, become the universal bouldering language used by today's up-and-coming boulderers. The magazines use it, many books use it, and now it makes its way into this text. Since the V system was established in the early 1990s at Hueco Tanks, Texas (soon after the first comprehensive bouldering guides such as *Colorado Front Range Bouldering* were published in America), many people have taken up bouldering as a favorite pastime.

Today, bouldering has quadrupled in popularity. The rating system below should be self-evident and can be gauged with reference to the classic Yosemite Decimal System. Although the V system is *en vogue,* in large part due to its higher numbers of comparison, boulderers must take a lighthearted approach to bouldering with each other. It is a difficult task to create a consistently accurate grade without an ascent consensus. Usually when a route is completed, the first ascensionist tacks on a grade based on his or her experience with the grading scale and the level at which they climb within it. This is more or less a suggested grade, and until other climbers repeat the problem and a general consensus is gathered, the original grade holds. After other people climb it, the grade of the route may be pushed up or down. Many of the grades in this book are only tentative grades because many of these problems have been climbed by only one person. A problem may feel harder for some and easier for others, depending on one's height, arm-span, leg-span, etc. Over time, you should get a general feel for the grading scale presented and be able to make your own decisions; the grades are only there to give you a general sense of the difficulty. Gradings can be used to classify but really should not be taken too seriously. The heart of bouldering is found in exploration and personal challenge. Greatness of physical and mental strength is measured in its essence through compassion and vision. Do not be offended by whatever grading system a person chooses to use for his or her problems. As many of us have said in the past, the best thing that can happen to a rating system is learning not to have to use it at all. For all I care, you could rate problems "good," "way good," and "no f-ing way." Have fun!

RELATIVE BOULDERING SCALES

Yosemite	V system	B System	Fontainebleau
	V0	B5.8	
	V0	B5.9	
5.10a/b	V0	B5.10	
5.10c/d	V1	B5.10+	5c
5.11a/b	V2	B1-	
5.11c/d	V3	B1	6a
5.12a	V4	B1	6b
5.12b	V5	B1+	6c
5.12c/d	V6	B2-	6c
5.13a	V7	B2	7a
5.13b	V8	B2	7b
5.13c/d	V9	B2+	7b+
5.14a	V10	B2+	7c
5.14b	V11	B2+	7c+
5.14c	V12	B2+	8a
5.14d	V13	B3	8b
5.15a	V14	B3	8b+

ACCESS

All of the areas covered in this book are on public land and fall within the jurisdiction of city parks, state parks, or federal Bureau of Land Management. All of these agencies have statutes and regulations regarding public access and activities. It is important to become familiar with these rules, since they vary somewhat from one area to the other. Flagstaff Mountain and Eldorado Canyon are the only areas that require an entrance fee, although Flagstaff is free if you live in Boulder County.

A few of the areas described in this book have seasonal raptor closures. The closures at present are in effect from February 1st through July 31st. These areas are the Third Flatiron, Sacred Cliffs, Skunk Canyon, Fern Canyon, and Shadow Canyon. Find alternate destinations during these times. Get updates from authorities, because the closures are sometimes lifted early. There are some areas on the Front Range that were relatively popular bouldering areas in the 1960s but have since become privately owned. As time goes on, more and more of the landscape will be consumed by contractors for homes and business development. Hopefully, the areas in this book will forever remain public domain. In the meantime, respect the environment and enjoy the access to it.

The areas in this book were set aside for the preservation and enjoyment of the natural environment. Already these areas are feeling the effects of their ever-growing popularity. As responsible outdoor participants, it is our duty to help preserve these beautiful areas through removal of existing litter and by staying on the trails or footpaths as much as possible. Many of the bouldering areas described in this book are used and treasured by a diverse public, most of whom do not boulder. Have some consideration and lend a helping hand by keeping these places at least as nice as you found them.

WEATHER

The weather in Boulder, Colorado, is good for a great majority of the year. Since most of the bouldering is found at a fairly low elevation, if the sun is shining it is usually warm. If it happens to snow, just wait a few days and when the sun reappears it is sure to dry the rocks. Colorado winters usually host at least one short period of extended cold or rain, which occurs in late winter to early spring. The fall and spring normally have the best bouldering weather, although on a nice winter day in Colorado conditions could not be better.

SAFETY

Bouldering usually causes injury in the form of pulled tendons and twisted ankles. Avoiding this is very simple. Use a rope that is securely anchored if you feel that there is any chance that you may hurt yourself if you fall. Warming up and progressing slowly helps prevent injury to the joints, tendons, and muscles. Concentrating on safety is key to a long life of fun bouldering. Bouldering with a partner inevitably provides incentive to push each other's ability as well as providing the confidence of a good spot. The spotter should stand behind the boulderer and be prepared for a possible slip or miss. The role of the spotter is **not** to catch the falling climber; instead, it is to properly realign the feet of the falling climber with the landing zone, perhaps also in some small way allowing a gentler landing. Particular attention should be paid to protecting the falling climber's head. When working together properly, a spotter and boulderer take off a little bit of the psychological edge. For the problems that are "highball" an (**hb**) is given. If the problem is seriously dangerous as well as highball an (**xhb**) is given. Only a small percentage of the boulder problems in this book are given such ratings.

EQUIPMENT

One of the true pleasures of bouldering is the simplicity of gear needed. A pair of shoes and a chalk bag are usually enough to please most boulderers. At times, a toprope may be employed for those problems that are too highball to be safe. Today, many boulderers carry along with them a crash pad. This lightweight, backpacked unit is a good thing to have and will ultimately help prevent bodily injury and harm. To order the Meadow Maroon custom crash pad and chalk bag designed by Bob Horan, call Horangutan at (303) 447-3064 or write to P.O. Box 7218, Boulder, CO 80306.

FLATIRONS OVERVIEW

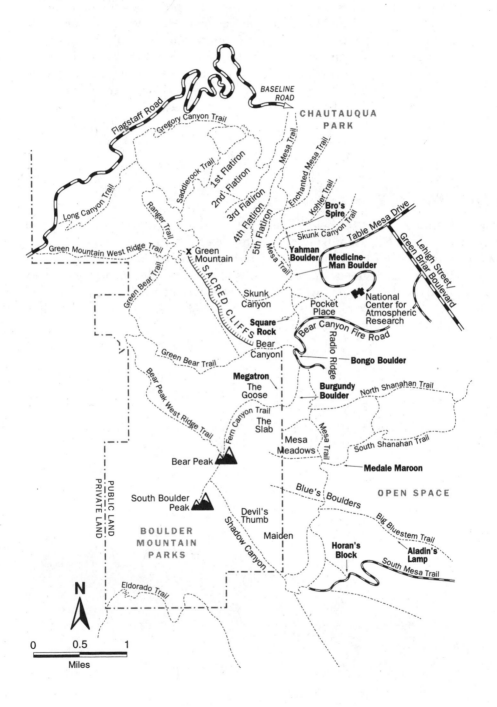

Mount Sanitas

This spiney ridge of west-facing outcrops is filled with moderate boulder problems that have good landings. A short hike uphill to the ridge takes you to a pine-scented sandstone bouldering area featuring enough rock to please all levels of ability. (See map on page 8.)

Directions: To reach Mount Sanitas you must locate Colorado Highway 93 (Broadway) in Boulder. Take Broadway to Mapleton Street, just north of the Pearl Street Mall downtown. Take Mapleton west toward the mountains. The small city park with its pavilion and fire pit is located about half a block west of Memorial Hospital at the base of the foothills. Park near the shelter and walk north over a footbridge, following the trail around to the west (left) and uphill until you reach the main ridge. This north-stretching ridge is filled with cracks, faces, and arêtes and makes an enjoyable after-work place to go. Just look along the walls for the chalk marks to find the many well-tracked problems this fun place has to offer.

History: The history of Mount Sanitas bouldering is accredited to a wide variety of climbers. Many local and traveling climbers have come through this bouldering area

- (A) Ridge Gap Wall
- (B) Classy Wall
- (C) Corner Block
- (D) Twin Fins
- (E) Leaning Overhang
- (F) North Shelf Blocks
- (G) South Shelf Block
- (H) Sanitas Proper

Mount Sanitas from the west.

MOUNT SANITAS

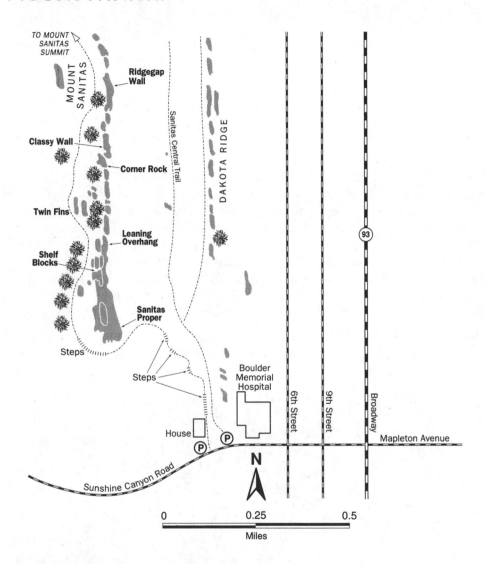

TO MOUNT
SANITAS
SUMMIT

MOUNT SANITAS

Ridgegap
Wall

Classy Wall

Corner Rock

Sanitas Central Trail

DAKOTA RIDGE

Twin Fins

Leaning
Overhang

Shelf
Blocks

Sanitas
Proper

Steps

Steps

Boulder
Memorial
Hospital

House

93

6th Street

9th Street

Broadway

Mapleton Avenue

N

Sunshine Canyon Road

0   0.25   0.5

Miles

Sanitas Proper

North Shelf Blocks

to enjoy its dakota sandstone offerings. Local boulderers such as Eric Doub, Skip Guerin, and Bob Horan—to name a few—have explored much of the potential within the Sanitas area.

SANITAS PROPER

This is the first wall encountered when hiking around to the north from up the trail. Chalk should be apparent. This formation extends from the lower southeast and continues up the slope.

   1. Improper Traverse V0 Traverse the base of the spired rock.

   2. Arête Crack V2 Self-explanatory route on the left side of the spire.

SOUTH SHELF BLOCK

This is the chalked wall immediately left of the Arête Crack.

NORTH SHELF BLOCKS

This block is located on the shelf just above the South Shelf Block. Continue a short ways uphill to access this interesting shelf of fine dakota sandstone. Walk onto the shelf.

Leaning Overhang

1. **Shelving Traverse V2** Traverse the blocks from north to south.
2. **The Layaway V1** Climb up the face on the far-left side via laybacks.
3. **Bulging Crack V2 (hb)** Climb up the crack and over the bulge.
4. **Tree Left Face V1** Climb the face just left of the tree, right of the *Bulging Crack*.
5. **V0 Corner V0** Climb the face and corner right of the tree.
6. **V0 Slot V0** Climb the slot right of the Corner.

NORTH SHELF BLOCK (SOUTH END)

This block is somewhat connected to the North Shelf Block and located on the shelf to the south.

7. **Face the Right V0** Climb the face up the middle of the block to its highest point.

LEANING OVERHANG ROCK

From the North Shelf Blocks, walk up and around to the north, to the east side of the Sanitas Proper. This excellent bouldering apparatus is found hanging on an eastern shelf and has great landings.

1. **The Leaning Overhang V5 (B1+)** Climb out the overhang to the right, utilizing the best edges available. Other eliminates are also worthwhile.

TWIN FINS

Continue upslope, a short ways from the Sanitas Proper and its North and South Shelf Blocks, along the trail, and you can't miss these classic dakota fins. One sits to the right of the trail (the lower fin), and one sits above and behind the other. Both offer great fun.

Leha Nickie on The Flake (V0) on the East Fin, and Terri Nickie on the Other One (V1) on the West Fin, Twin Fins, Mount Sanitas.

Twin Fins

Corner Block

EAST FIN

This fin is located just behind and to the east of the West Fin.

1. **Traverser V1** Traverse the wall.
2. **Flake V0** Climb up the layback system.
3. **Face V0** Climb up the middle of the face.
4. **Face Route V0** Climb up the far-right side of the fin.

WEST FIN

This is the westernmost fin along the trail.

1. **Traverse Fin V2** Traverse the lower portion of the fin.
2. **Undercling Fin V0** Start off the undercling and climb up the left side of the face.
3. **Crack in the Fin V0** Climb the crack on its west face.
4. **Other One V1** Climb the face immediately right of the *Crack in the Fin*.
5. **Right One V0** Climb the face on the far-right side.

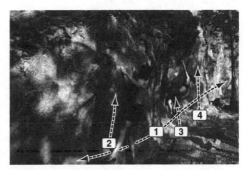

Classy Wall   *Ridge Gap Wall*

CORNER BLOCK

Hike a short ways up the trail from the fins and you come to this blocky spire of dakota on the right side of the trail.

1. **Overhanger V3** Climb the steep face on the far-left side of the block.
2. **The Prow V2** Climb the prow of the block.
3. **Bulgy V0** Climb the far-right bulge of the block.

CLASSY WALL

Immediately up from and behind the Corner Block, you see this sheer-edged wall.

1. **Central Left V1** Climb up the left side of the wall.
2. **Central Right V1** Climb up the right side of the wall.

RIDGE GAP WALL

Continue hiking uptrail for a short distance and you run into this wall sitting right next to the trail. It has an elongated west face with a great traverse just off the ground.

1. **The Traverse V1** Traverse the wall from right to left and back again.
2. **Left Most V0** Climb the face on the far-left side of the wall.
3. **V-Block V0** Climb up the face utilizing the block.
4. **Seam Way V0** Follow the seam.

DAKOTA RIDGE

This alternate destination is visible just east of Mount Sanitas. The spiney, hogback ridge is full of bouldering and toprope problems for all levels of ability. Crack, face, corner, and arête-filled, isolated formations offer a wide variety of challenges with a high-over-Boulder view from the north edge of the city. Many local climbers have enjoyed the variety of good problems that are offered by this intermittently good dakota sandstone ridge.

BOULDER CANYON

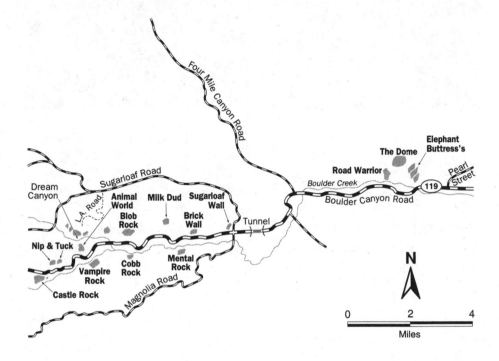

BOULDER CANYON

Boulder Canyon is rich with fine granite and offers a large number of single- and multi-pitch routes, but boulder fields of this quality granite are limited. The well-known bouldering that exists in Boulder Canyon is found at the base of the larger formations. Castle Rock hosts several classic problems such as *Acrobat Overhang* and *The Gill Crack*. The Nip and Tuck Rocks offer the *Barrio Traverse*. Look for other problems along the canyon on isolated blocks and boulders just above the canyon's road. These blocks and boulders offer excellent problems that are sure to please any serious boulderer.

Directions: To reach Boulder Canyon, locate Colorado Highway 93 (Broadway in Boulder) and take it to Canyon Boulevard. At Canyon, head west toward the mountains and straight into Boulder Canyon. The mileage count begins at the Elephant Buttress (0.0 mile), the first major formation encountered on the right (north) side of the road. Castle Rock is up the road 11.9 miles from the Elephant Buttress.

History: Much of the problems described here are the work of John Gill, Chris Jones, Bob Horan, Skip Guerin, Charlie Bentley, Jay Droeger, and many other local boulderers.

ROAD WARRIOR ROCK

As you enter Boulder Canyon, there is a large four-point buttress on the right (north) side of the road called the Elephant Buttress. To the northwest of this buttress there is a prominent granite dome appropriately named The Dome. Just past these granite masses there are two road cuts. Park at the far west end of the second road cut and look at its west face to find this overhanging crack, located just off the deck.

1. **The Road Warrior V5 (hb)** Climb the crack out the overhang. A spotter is seriously suggested.

Road Warrior Rock

15

Sugarloaf Wall

SUGARLOAF WALL

After the first and only tunnel up Boulder Canyon, there are two main turnoffs. The first is Magnolia Road, heading south (left), followed soon thereafter by Sugarloaf Road (to the right, or north). Take Sugarloaf Road approximately 100 feet to an overhanging wall just off the left side of the road.

1. **Leaning Shelf V3** Climb up the overhang just off the road to the shelf above, exit left.

2. **The Falling One V6 (hb)** From the back of the overhang, climb up and out to the left utilizing a semi-dyno to good edges, exit left.

NIP AND TUCK

Approximately 10.6 miles uproad from The Elephant Buttress, on the right (north) side you encounter Nip and Tuck. These two masses are separated by a gully that separates the western mass (Nip) from the eastern one (Tuck).

NIP

This is the western formation. Nip has an excellent face route on the left edge of the south face.

1. **Gill's Bulges V5** Climb the sloping holds.

The Barrio

Tuck

THE BARRIO

At the far-left side of the Nip rock, behind the guardrail look for a severely overhanging roof system with good-looking holds skirting diagonally to the upper, right.

    1. The Barrio Traverse V7 Start on the lower left end and traverse up to the right. Other variations exist.

TUCK

This is the eastern formation, with a prominent overhanging, sheer wall with crack and arête.

    1. Caddis V10 (hb) Climb the granite, right-leaning seam, left of the arête, through the bulge to the face above. Follow the bolts.

    2. Touch Me I'm Sick V7 (hb) Climb the severely overhanging east wall, utilizing the arête and crack. This problem requires incredible state-of-the-art moves.

Castle Rock, Acrobat Overhang

Castle Rock, Gill Crack

CASTLE ROCK

This large island formation lies between the north side of Boulder Creek and the south side of the road, about 11.9 miles uproad from the Elephant Buttress. Hang a left around the west end of the rock and locate the large south face. John Gill established many daring feats on this sheer granite bouldering wall.

1. **The Acrobat Overhang V5 (B1+)** This is a problem of sheer finger strength. A doorjamb fingertip hang is practically necessary to pull this one off. Located on the far-left side of the south face.

2. **The Gill Crack V5 (hb)** Today most people toprope this and for a good reason. The crack is on the southwest face of Castle Rock, at the base of the wall, to the right of the *Acrobat Overhang*. Walk up a short slope from the dirt road and see this incredible crack.

FLAGSTAFF MOUNTAIN

When visiting or living in the picturesque city of Boulder, Colorado, one should not miss the historic boulders of Flagstaff Mountain. The easy access by car has made this natural playground an area favorite. Spread out magically amidst the pine-scented, forested slopes is an awesome array of short, demanding problems for all levels of ability. The conglomerate sandstone boulders often resemble mini-Flatiron formations that are usually quite solid. Flakes, pockets, edges, pebbles, and crystals appear on the well-rounded rocks to create an unlimited variety of challenges. Many climbers have found this exciting area to be a little rough on the fingertips at first, but with a bit of conditioning the fingers will begin to adapt by forming nice calluses. Flagstaff has been the training ground for many of the area's top climbers. With the strength and endurance gained on these small outcroppings, the standards of fifth-class roped climbs in the area have greatly advanced. Difficult rock climbing is enhanced through the development of bouldering skills. Flagstaff has an abundance of these state-of-the-art problems. (See map on page 20.)

Directions: To find this bouldering area, locate Baseline Road, which runs east-west through the city of Boulder. Go west on Baseline until you reach the foot of Flagstaff Mountain. From here, Baseline takes a sharp curve up and to the north and turns into Flagstaff Road. The mileage markings used in this book begin at a small bridge, located where the road curves to the north at the base of the mountain. A pleasant foot trail leads up the mountain and is located just past this bridge on the west side of the road. A daily parks pass is now required for non-local visitors.

History: Many climbers have frequented Flagstaff Mountain over the years, but many of the problems developed on the mountain are the work of climbers such as Pat Ament, John Gill, Paul Hagan, Bob Poling, Bob Williams, Eric Varney, Corwin Simmons, Larry Dalke, Ray Northcut, Layton Kor, Bob Culp, and Richard Smith in the 1950s and 1960s. In the 1970s, climbers such as Bob Candelaria, Jim Holloway, Neil Kaptain, and Dan Stone developed some finger-wrenching problems. In the 1980s and 1990s climbers such as Skip Guerin, Christian Griffith, Jerry Moffatt, and Bob Horan, to name just a few, put up, as well as repeated, many difficult problems and traverses.

FLAGSTAFF MOUNTAIN

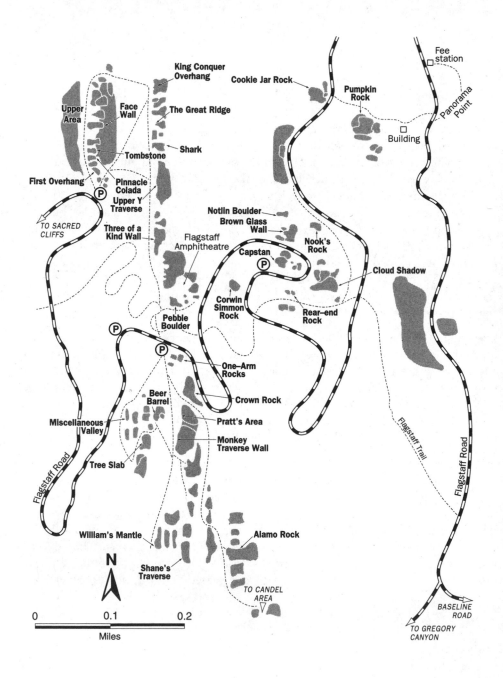

Pumpkin Rock

Cookie Jar Rock

PUMPKIN ROCK

This large blob-like boulder sits on the west side of the road southwest of the Panorama Point parking area. Many little problems are found all around its base. Two steel eye-bolts on top provide convenient toproping, and a ramp on the south side gives easy access to its summit. Many excellent high problems are to be found on its northwest face.

1. **North Face V3 (hb)** Climb the old aid line via pin scars and exit right.
2. **West Face Left V1** This climbs a scoop-like face to the right of the *North Face.*
3. **West Face Right V1** This climbs an overhanging wall to the right of the *West Face Left.*

COOKIE JAR ROCK

This is another prominent Flagstaff boulder which sits on the western side of the road, 0.8 mile up, a short way past the Flagstaff House Restaurant. Many classic problems are found on this formation. The south crack that splits this spire is probably one of the most climbed routes in the Boulder region. There are steel eye-bolts on top.

1. **Commitment V2** On the west side of the north face there is a bulge problem.
2. **Russian's Nose V1** Climb the overhang left of *Cookie Jar Crack.* There are several variations to this route.
3. **Cookie Jar Crack V0 (hb)** An excellent beginner's toprope found on the south side of the Cookie Jar.
4. **Rough One V3** Just below the *Cookie Jar Crack* and to the right is a roadcut block with an overhang leading to a short dihedral.

CLOUD SHAWDOW AREA

CAPSTAN ROCK

On the north side of the road, about 1.5 miles up Flagstaff Road, in the center of a hairpin turn, there is this prominent spire with a pointy summit and an obvious curving crack on its south face. Numerous great problems of various length and difficulty make this rock one of the many sought-after boulders on the mountain. Descend on the north side, careful of the road.

1. **Northwest Edges V2** This overhanging problem climbs off the edge of the road and up the northwest face via small edges. The rounded top requires a committing summit move.

2. **West Face V1 (hb)** This ascends the west face of Capstan with some interesting pockets and layaways.

3. **South Crack V2 (hb)** This ascends the obvious finger crack on the south face of the rock via pin scars from an early-'50s aid ascent.

4. **South Overhang V2-V4** This climbs the bulge just to the right of *South Crack*. A few variations have been done on this bulge. One reaches left off a hole to a sloping edge, another reaches up statically to the right off a crystal and a hole and another problem lunges off the holds up to the left or right.

5. **Just Right V7** This climbs the severe overhang to the right of the *South Overhang*. Pull onto the face with layaway moves, then reach with your right hand avoiding the pocket to the small holds at top. The top moves offer some delicate thin-edged balance moves.

6. **Diverse Traverse V2–V5** This fingery traverse moves along the bottom of the rock from an undercling at *Just Right* all the way past *South Crack* to the *North-*

Capstan Rock

Notlim Boulder

west Edges route, then back, if your endurance allows. The small finger holes are reminiscent of climbing at Buoux in France.

NOTLIM BOULDER

Down the slope to the north of Road Sign Rock there is an interesting boulder with a very bizarre route up its northern face.

1. **Hollow's Way V8** Fingertip your way up this desperate overhanging barn door layback.

REAR-END ROCK (NOT PICTURED)

From Capstan Rock, walk south, downhill, and a short way east along the main trail, to find this split boulder.

1. **Left Bulge V4** Climb the bulging face left of the crack via a tricky mantel.

2. **Crack Crack V3** This jams the south crack of the formation.

CLOUD SHADOW

At the first hairpin curve, a few feet up the road from Capstan and below the road to the southeast, you see this incredible formation. A very unique traverse with solution pockets is located on the formation's south face, as well as several difficult, bulging face problems.

CLOUD SHADOW (EAST END)

1. **Bob's Pull V5** Halfway across *Cloud Shadow Traverse* look for a nice circular pocket that you can cram both hands into. From here, place your left foot up onto a polished down-sloping ramp and crank in a dynamic motion up and slightly left for a large solution pocket.

2. **Cloud Shadow Traverse V4** There are a few different ways to traverse this wall, one staying fairly high across the pockets, and one staying very low. From *Consideration*, traverse to the left until you cannot hold on any longer.

3. **Lower Bulge Traverse V9** From *Contemplation* to *East Inside Corner*, this demanding traverse may be the hardest traverse Flagstaff has to offer.

4. **Contemplation V2 (hb)** Follow a seam curving to the left, then proceed with caution straight above.

5. **Moderate Bulge V0** Right of the *Lower Bulge Traverse* at the far-right, east-end of the formation, grab a large hole, get this as an undercling and make a long extended reach to the top.

6. **Reverse Consideration V4** This is the same as *Consideration*, except that you switch hands in the hole and reach up with the other hand. A whole different balance point is created with this move.

7. **Consideration V3 (B1)** On the right side of the wall, left of the bulge routes, at

Cloud Shadow (east end)

another bulging section is the deep hole. From the hole, reach up to a good edge with your right hand, then up to a sharp smaller edge with your left, then reach to the top of the angling shelf.

8. **Trice V10** Just right of *Consideration* is a sloping finger pocket approximately eight feet up in an overhanging bulge.

9. **Bob's Bulge V5** Right of *Consideration* and *Trice* is a prominent bulge above an undercling. Throw a heel over the bulge and proceed up the traversing shelf.

10. **East Inside Corner V0** On the far-east side of the traversing wall there is a small corner.

CLOUD SHADOW (WEST END)

1. **Launching Pad V4** On the very far-left side of the wall there is a difficult reach problem that launches off a small crystal up to a finger edge. Since the first ascent, the crystal has broken, creating a new challenge.

2. **Dandy Line V5** This strenuous problem climbs the steep face right of *Launching Pad*, and just left of *Hagan's Wall* via a small pebble.

3. **Hagan's Wall V5 (B1+)** Right of *Dandy Line* there is another bulging wall with a small flake for one hand and a solution pocket that fits two fingers for the other. Crank off the small boulder to a sloping hold above and work this to the top.

4. **Miar's Face V6** Ascend this strenuous, overhanging face just right of *Hagan's Wall*.

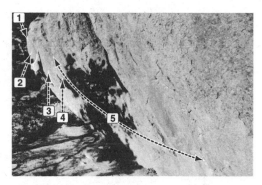

Cloud Shadow (west end)

5. Hand Traverse V2 On the left side of *Cloud Shadow Traverse*, right of *Hagan's Wall,* there is a left-angling ramp leading upward. Hand traverse this to a difficult reach out left.

THE ALCOVE

Slightly uphill behind the south face of Cloud Shadow Rock there is an alcove with some very excellent problems.

1. Sailor's Delight V1 (hb) This is located up above the alcove on a prominent bulging roof.

2. East Overhang V2 This is an obvious roof problem on the west side of the alcove.

3. Crack Allegro V1 Below *Sailor's Delight*, on a north-facing wall in the alcove, there is this right-leaning crack.

4. Allegro Bulge V2 This climbs the bulge right of *Crack Allegro* to a mantel on the top.

The Alcove

The Alcove

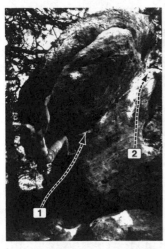

One Arm Rocks

Golf Club Boulder

GOLF CLUB BOULDER

On the far-east end of Cloud Shadow there is a prominent blob that looks like a golf club when looking at it from the west.

1. **The Angler V2** This is a strenuous hand-and-finger traverse from the east side of the blob to the far south side.

2. **The Roof V1** On the west side there is an overhang which is surmounted via a heel hook.

PRATT'S OVERHANG AREA

ONE ARM ROCKS

These two boulders sit together just off the road on the south side, after a sharp curve 1.6 miles up Flagstaff road. Many variations ascend these fun boulders which are mostly known for their steep one-arm problems.

1. **One-Arm Overhang V3** On the east rocks, west-facing overhang there is a one-arm problem that climbs into the small dihedral above the overhang.

2. **Right Hand Mantle V2** This one-arm problem climbs the north face of the west rock using a small crystal as a foothold while pressing into a one-arm mantel off a small edge.

Pratt's Overhang

PRATT'S OVERHANG

From the One Arm Rocks, walk a few hundred feet along a path leading south from the parking area and you soon discover this west-facing, overhanging formation with several classic problems.

1. **Pratt's Mantle V2** This is most directly done as a straightforward mantel, although many variations using small edges have also been accomplished.

2. **Aerial Burial V3** From some small holds below the shelf on *Pratt's Mantle*, double lunge up for the shelf. Variations do exist.

3. **Pratt's Overhang V2** To the right of the mantel shelf there is a right-slanting slot. Climb this via some awkward moves. Many variations exist.

4. **Stone Ground V3** This climbs the face between *Pratt's Overhang* and *Smith's Overhang*.

5. **Smith's Overhang V5 (B1-)** To the right of *Pratt's Overhang* is a severely thin overhanging face with a prominent layback flake.

6. **Gill Swing V4** This is a super-dynamic move that goes off a small layback hold right of *Smith's Overhang* and shoots for the top.

7. **Crystal Corner V2** Just right of *Smith's Overhang* is a small overhanging arête with a prominent crystal on it. Layback the corner to the crystal, then move up to the top via a high step.

8. **Gully V0** To the right of *Crystal Corner* is a gully which can be mantled or face climbed.

MONKEY TRAVERSE AREA

Farther down the trail, south of Pratt's Overhang Area, is a sunny west-facing, overhanging outcrop with a variety of traverses and roof problems. This is probably the most popular area of all of the Flagstaff Boulders. When first arriving at Flagstaff it is a good place to get the local beta, becoming familiar with the rock, and perhaps meet a climbing partner.

1. **Monkey Traverse V4** This is the obvious chalked-up traverse that goes from right to left and back again. Your endurance will grow the more you apply yourself to this routine. Many other contrived variations on this traverse exist, some very hard.

2. **West Overhang V1 (hb)** Just slightly left of the *Monkey Traverse* midsection there is an obvious roof problem.

3. **Million Dollar Spider V4** On the far south end of the traverse there are a few overhanging problems. Grab for a pinch in the overhang and reach for the top.

Monkey Traverse

Beer Barrel

BEER BARREL

From the parking area 1.6 miles up Flagstaff Road, where the trail that leads to Pratt's Overhang Area goes straight, drop down to the southwest until you see a picnic table. Just west of this table is the Beer Barrel rock. Many incredible problems and rock formations lie beyond.

1. **West Traverse V3** On the west face of the Beer Barrel there is a great overhanging flake system. Traverse this back and forth for a good pump.

2. **Southwest Corner V0** This classic layback system is a very enjoyable problem.

3. **South Face V0** Climb the good edges up the south face to an overhanging bulge crack. Several other variations on the south face of the rock are possible.

4. **Pinch Pebble V5** This climbs to the left of the *Polling Pebble Route* using only two pebbles.

5. **Polling Pebble Route V5 (B/+)** This climbs the bulge on the southeast corner of the formation via some very small holds where the famous pebble used to exist. This pebble was the largest on the face and withstood 30 years of pulling before it was pulled off.

DISTANT DANCER PINNACLE

This is the pointy spire just southwest of the Beer Barrel. Easy access to its summit is found on its north face.

1. **West Overhang V1–V4** Many variations on the west side of the pinnacle are possible. Start as low as possible in the shelf.

2. **Red Horn Overhang V1** On the southwest side of the spire is an overhanging corner. Layback this corner up to summit.

3. **Distant Dancer 5.12 V6 (xhb)** This exciting problem ascends the south face of the spire via laybacks, underclings, and long reaches with a swing. The route was first toproped and then later bouldered out by Bob Horan in 1982.

Bulging Crack Wall

Distant Dancer Pinnacle

TREE SLAB

Down the hill to the south of Distant Dancer Pinnacle is a smooth west-facing slab with many great problems up it.

1. **Classic Line V0** Behind the tree is an obvious face. This was done one-handed in the '60s.

2. **Layback Crack V0** Right of the tree is a fun layback crack with a small challenge.

3. **Slab Traverse V0** Move across this traverse of the slab one-handed for an excellent challenge. It is hardest if the climber stays close to the ground.

MISCELLANEOUS VALLEY

This group of formations is located below, and to the north of the Tree Slab. The west-facing rocks have many good problems.

BULGING CRACK WALL

From the Beer Barrel, hike around to the north to the trail below. This wall sits on the north edge of the outcrop along the lower trail.

1. **Left Bulge V0** To the left of the crack there is this enjoyable bulge problem.

2. **Leaning Jam V1** This is the crack out of the bulge on the left side of the wall.

THE ALAMO ROCK AREA

South of Crown Rock and southeast, above the *Monkey Traverse* there is a foot path leading to the south following the summit ridgeway. After about 50 yards, the large Alamo Rock formation comes into view with its rounded summit and overhanging west side. The east face resembles a Flatiron-like slab, offering moderate access to its summit.

Tree Slab

The Rib Boulder *Bulging Wall*

THE RIB BOULDER

Below, and slightly northwest of Alamo Rock there is a small cubical boulder with some fun routes on its sides.

1. **The Crease V0** Climb the flaky crease on the west end of the boulder.
2. **Arête It V1** Climb the arête on the southwest corner.
3. **Face It V0** Climb the face to the right of the arête.

BULGING WALL

Just east of the Rib Boulder is a bulging wall with a prominent finger crack. This sits below Alamo Rock and is connected to its lower northwest face.

1. **Bulging Face V1** Left of the finger crack is a bulging face route.
2. **Dalke Finger Crack V1** Climb the finger and hand crack in the wall.
3. **Rib Right V0** Right of the finger crack is a nice face with good holds.
4. **Arrows Traverse V4** Go back and forth along the lower portion of the Bulging Wall.
5. **Diamond Face V3** Below the overhanging crack on the west face of the Alamo Rock, immediately to the northwest, there is a vertical south-facing wall with small edges.

THE CANDEL AREA

This is a ridge of broken boulders and slabs southeast of Alamo Rock. Hike up and behind Alamo Rock and head south along the summit ridge.

THE JUG

Follow a faint trail south along the ridge, south of *Alamo Rock*, to a dead tree—a formation with a finger crack on its west side is located to the right of this dead tree. From this crack hike to the south around the corner. The Jug is a west-facing wall with a gray ramp rock on its left.

Diamond Face

The Jug

1. **The Ramp V1** Climb the southwest-facing, narrow gray slab.
2. **Red Streak V1** On the northwest face there is a red-streaked wall. Climb this to the top.

SUNSHINE SLAB (NOT PICTURED)
Just to the right and farther downhill is a large southwest-facing slabby wall.
1. **Michael's Face V2** Directly behind the tree is a thin face with crystals.

GREAT RIDGE AREA

THE PEBBLE WALL
From the parking area around the curve from Crown Rock, 1.6 miles up Flagstaff Road, walk uphill to the north on the Flagstaff Trail for a few hundred feet. Look in the trees on the right to find this incredible well-rounded boulder. Many pebbles and crystals lace the walls.
1. **North Face V0** This problem skirts left of the *North Overhang*, avoiding its crux moves.
2. **North Overhang V3** On the north side there is a prominent overhang with many pebbles.
3. **West Overhang V3** On the northwest edge there is a climb up a prow.
4. **Southwest Corner V0** This laybacks the rounded corner up from the *Southwest Face*.
5. **Over Yourself Traverse V10** Traverse the lower portion of the south and west face.

The Pebble Wall

6. **Southwest Face V3** Another delicate face with a little more exposure.

7. **High Step V1** On the right side of the *Direct South Face*, there is another pebbly face.

8. **Direct South Face V3 (B1)** Right of the *High Step*, left of the mantel crystal there is a steep pebbly face that starts off a root.

9. **Crystal Mantel V2** There are several ways to mantel this obvious large crystal on the far-right side of the south face.

10. **Original Route V0** On the southeast corner of the boulder there is a face ending with an undercling. Start near the small boulder.

NORTH ROCKS

Just east of the Pebble Wall there are two boulders with an unlimited variety of good problems.

1. **Left Rock V0** Climb up the middle of the west face of the northernmost rock.

2. **Right Rock V1** Climb up the left side of the southernmost rock via slopey crystals.

THE RED WALL

Just behind and to the east of the North Rocks there is an interesting, smooth, south-facing vertical wall with very small edges on it. Some of Flagstaff's hardest problems lie on this wall.

North Rocks

The Red Wall

1. **Left Side V1** Climb the far-left side via a small finger pocket.

2. **Center Left V3** This tight move reaches up for an obvious hole with your right hand and then extends for a pinch crystal.

3. **Standard Route V3** Instead of reaching the hole with your right hand, try it with your left.

4. **Direct V5** Just right of the *Standard Route* there is a difficult problem that starts with a small pebble for your left hand and a dish or cup hold for your right. Reach up to a good edge then a small finger niche.

5. **Right Side V4 (B1)** On the right side of the wall, near a tree, there is this classic hard problem that goes off a cup with your left hand to a long reach to a crystal niche with your right.

6. **Far-right Side V3** Just behind the tree there is a face problem that reaches over from the right to the holds atop the *Right Side* route.

THE FLAGSTAFF AMPHITHEATRE
This enclosed outcropping can be found just to the north of the Pebble Wall and is packed with many splendid problems.

RIGHT SIDE ROCK
This is the rock found on the right (east) side of the two Amphitheatre Rocks. All problems exit up and to the left.

1. **The Overhanging Hand Traverse V1** Follow the large finger holds up and right.

2. **Gill Direct V4 (B1)** From some small edges right of *Overhanging Hand Traverse*, ascend up and slightly right to some good holds at the lip.

3. **South Bulge V1** On the right side of the wall there are edged shelves leading to the top.

4. **South Corner V1** On the right side of the wall there is a short overhanging corner.

Skip Guerin boulders up the Center Left *(V3) on the Red Wall in the Flagstaff* *Amphitheatre.*

LEFT SIDE ROCK

This is the left side (south) rock that forms the Amphitheatre. (See photo page 37.)

1. **High Overhang V0 (hb)** On the far-left side, up the slot, there is a scary reach problem off a high boulder, which finishes by mantling the airy lip.

2. **South Face Left Side V3** An obvious corner/arête with some small edges.

3. **Finger Trip V5** A difficult mantel problem right of the *South Face Left-Side.*

4. **Briggs Route V3** Another thin pebbled face which starts up the leaning corner.

5. **Direct South Face V3** From the slab under the base, climb the small pebbles.

6. **Crystal Swing V2** A leap to a large pebble on the right side.

Left and Right Side Rocks

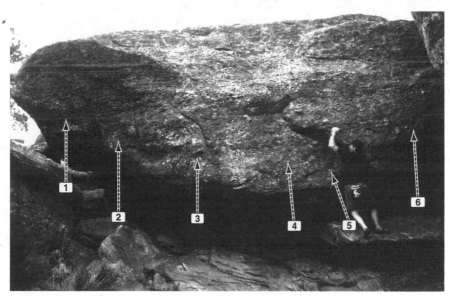

Left Side Rock

Overhang Wall, South
Undercling

Overhang Wall, Big Overhang

OVERHANG WALL

When leaving the Amphitheatre, head southwest and continue up the hill to the north to this wall of overhanging problems.

1. **South Undercling V3** At the lower south end of this formation, immediately down to the left of Left Side Rock, there is a steep face with an undercling.

2. **Big Overhang V2 (hb)** The problem climbs the large overhanging block on the north end of the formation and is uphill, around to the north of the Amphitheatre.

THE GREAT RIDGE

This is a series of west-facing overhanging walls and spires uphill to the north of the Overhang Wall and Pebble Wall. There are many classic problems here as well as some excellent traverses.

Three of a Kind Wall

THREE OF A KIND WALL

This is the first formation at the lower south end of the Great Ridge. You can play on three serious face problems and a low traverse here.

1. **The Face V3** On the left side of the west face there is a soft, high-quality sandstone face. Be careful of the loose flakes.

2. **Kaptain Face V5** Right of *The Face* route there is another thin face.

3. **Round Pebble V4 (hb)** Right of *Kaptain Face* there is another problem ascending a thin seam via laybacks on small edges to a good edge and pebble.

4. **High Flake V4 (hb)** On the right side, just to the left of a groove/trough, there is a prominent flake extending up and to the left. From the top of the flake reach up for a small crystal.

5. **The Groove V0** An obvious groove with a fun challenge.

6. **Bulging Slab V3** At the start of the Great Ridge, on the far-right side of Three of a Kind Wall, there is a sloping traverse that leads to a groove. This problem climbs up the sloping slab at the start of *The Traverse*.

7. **The Traverse V5** Start from the far-right side of the wall, traverse across to the flake.

Karen Roberts on the Upper Y-Traverse *(V3),* The Great Ridge.

The Great Ridge, north end overview

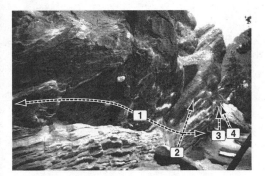

Upper Y-Traverse Wall

Shark's Rock

UPPER Y-TRAVERSE

Uphill from the Three of a Kind Wall there is another large outcropping with an overhanging west wall and a well-chalked traverse skirting its base. A Y-shaped crack is visible in the gap.

1. **Upper Y-Traverse V3** This great traverse is considered one of the best on Flagstaff.
2. **Y Right Face V0** Climb the big-hold face right of the Y-Slots.
3. **Pinch Bulge V3** At the far-right end of the wall there is a good finger flake in the overhang. From this flake, reach up with your left hand to a pinch layback on the arête, then reach for the top.
4. **Direct Mantle V4** Left of the pinch problem there is an obvious mantel shelf.

SHARK'S ROCK

Up from the *Upper Y-Traverse*, there is a spire with a vertical corner on its southwest face.

1. **Direct West V4** Climb up the middle of the west face.
2. **West Arête V3** Climb the southwest corner.

LITTLE FLATIRON

This describes the small spire just uphill to the north from Shark's Rock.

1. **Leany Face V1** This ascends the left overhanging face.
2. **Right Arête V3** This difficult problem takes the overhanging arête on the southwest corner.

King Conquer Rock

KING CONQUER ROCK

This is the large blocky formation at the top of the Great Ridge and is loaded with many excellent problems including a classic overhanging jam crack.

1. **King Conquer Overhang V3 (hb)** This is the overhanging crack that splits the block.

2. **Face Out V5 (B1+)** Right of the crack there is an overhanging face with very small, sharp edges.

3. **Southwest Layback V1** On the far-right side there is an overhanging layback.

4. **Conquer Traverse V6 (B2-)** This is a low traverse along the King Conquer formation.

First Overhang

Pinnacle Colada

THE UPPER AREA

This is the high point of the Flagstaff boulders, located up the road around a curve from Pratt Parking Area.

FIRST OVERHANG

At the second hairpin, uphill past the Crown Rock Parking Area, look for a classic boulder sitting at the northeast edge of a parking area.

1. **Masochism Tango V6** On the far-left side of the rock there is an overhanging arête.

2. **Center Route V7** The center of the face between *First Overhang* and *Masochism Tango*.

3. **First Overhang V5 (B1+)** This is a problem on the right side of the southwest face.

PINNACLE COLADA

This is the first prominent rectangular pinnacle uphill and to the north of the First Overhang boulder.

1. **Standard Route V0 (hb)** On the left side of the west face there is a right-leaning corner.

2. **Pebble Reach V3 (hb)** There is a steep face on the right side with a pebble high up.

3. **Southwest Corner V3** On the southwest corner of the formation there is a vertical arête.

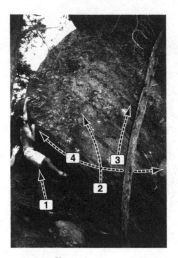

Tombstone Spire   *Face Wall*

4. **South Face V0** On the south face there is a short face problem with a good flake up top.

5. **Colada Traverse V4** Traverse across the overhang on the bottom of the pinnacle.

TOMBSTONE SPIRE

Just to the north of Pinnacle Colada is another, smaller rectangular pinnacle with good routes.

1. **Triple Bulge V2** On the northwest corner of the pinnacle there is an obvious bulging arête.

2. **West Side V0** On the west face of the pinnacle there is a good route with large holds.

3. **Southwest Bulge V1** Climb the southwest corner of the spire.

FACE WALL

Just north of the Tombstone there is a bouldering wall with trees very close to its south face.

1. **West Roof V1** On the west side there is an obvious overhang with little edges.

2. **Left Side V3 (hb)** On the left side of the south face there is a delicate face problem.

3. **Center V3 (hb)** On the south face of the wall there is a delicate face going up the middle.

4. **Horan's Traverse V6 (B2-)** Traverse across the lower wall from far-right to the left finishing with the *West Roof*.

West Ridge of Green Mountain (Sacred Cliffs)

This extensive, spiney band of blocks, spires, and boulders is located on the west ridge of Green Mountain. It is to the southwest of Flagstaff Mountain and west of the Fourth and Fifth Flatirons, Skunk Canyon, and Dinosaur Mountain.

Directions: Moderate access to these cliffs is gained by driving up Flagstaff Mountain Road (Baseline Road West) approximately 2.5 miles from the base of the mountain where Baseline Road meets the Gregory Canyon turnoff. Drive past the Flagstaff summit up toward Gross Reservoir. At the crest of the road, just after the final hairpin turn, you encounter the trailhead known as Green Mountain West Ridge. This trail, approximately 1 mile long, will take you directly up to the Northern Spine of the Sacred Cliffs. From a point just short of the summit, you can access the Trail Rocks, the Balarney Stones, the Land of Oz, the Sunset Blocks, Garden Wall, Eden Rocks, Stonehenge, and the Hobbit Area.

History: Ninety-five percent of the problems within the Maroon Garden were put up by Bob Horan from the beginning of the 1980s to the end of the 1990s.

SACRED CLIFFS—NORTHERN SPINE

The Sacred Cliffs are broken up into two sections seperated by a rockless saddle. The Northern Spine consists of smaller summit blocks and spires compared to the larger Southern Spine formations. Below the summit rocks of the Northern Spine there is an awesome array of quality blocks and boulders. Each bouldering area follows prominent fall lines of rock which have broken away from the summit rocks and tumbled downslope in a somewhat regular fashion. The bouldering areas, north to south, are the Trail Rocks, the Balarney Stones, the Land of Oz, Sunset Blocks, and Ridgebreak Boulders. Each are accessed by hiking the western slopes, very close to the summit ridges.

SACRED CLIFFS

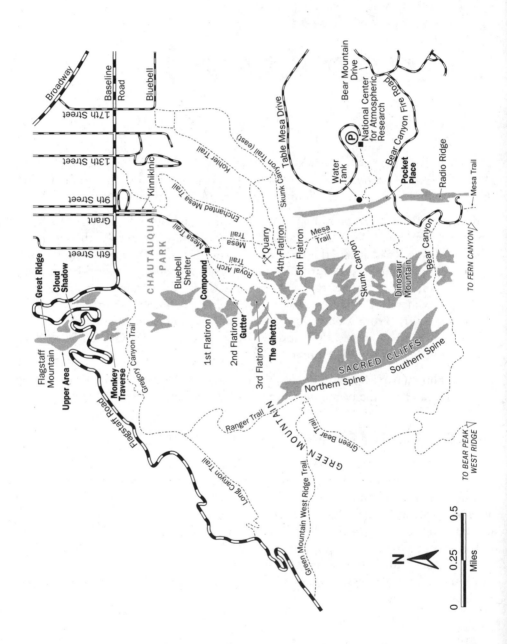

Sacred Cliffs (Maroon Garden)

SACRED CLIFFS DETAIL

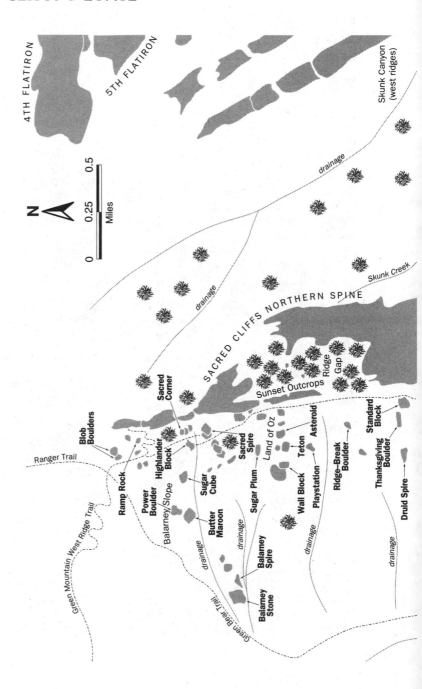

4TH FLATIRON

5TH FLATIRON

Skunk Canyon (west ridges)

N

0   0.25   0.5
Miles

drainage

Skunk Creek

SACRED CLIFFS NORTHERN SPINE

drainage

Sacred Corner

Sunset Outcrops

Ridge Gap

Standard Block

Blob Boulders

Ranger Trail

Highlander Block

Sacred Spire

Land of Oz

Asteroid

Teton

Ridge–Break Boulder

Thanksgiving Boulder

Ramp Rock

Power Boulder

Balarney/Slope

Sugar Cube

Butter Maroon

Sugar Plum

Wall Block

Playstation

Druid Spire

Green Mountain West Ridge Trail

drainage

drainage

Balarney Spire

Green Bear Trail

Balarney Stone

drainage

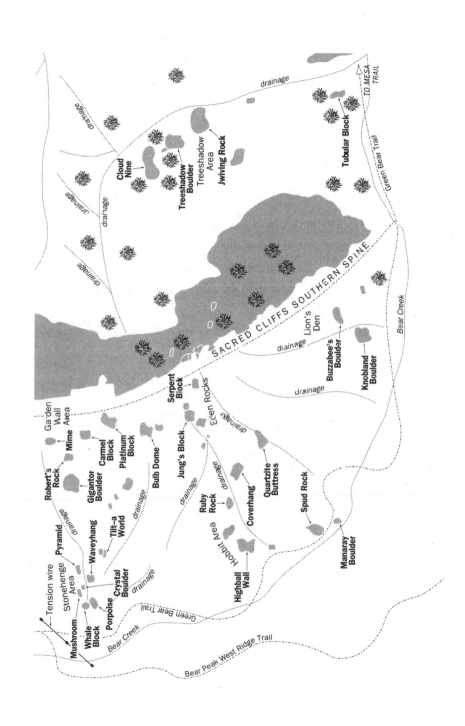

TO MESA TRAIL

drainage

Green Bear Trail

Tubular Block

Treeshadow Area

Jwiving Rock

Treeshadow Boulder

Cloud Nine

drainage

drainage

drainage

Bear Creek

SACRED CLIFFS SOUTHERN SPINE

Lion's Den

drainage

Buzzabee's Boulder

Knobland Boulder

drainage

Serpent Block

Ecen Rocks

Ga'den Wall Area

Mime

Robert's Rock

Carmel Block

Platinum Block

Bulb Dome

Jung's Block

Gigantor Boulder

drainage

drainage

Quartzite Buttress

Spud Rock

Tilt-a-World

Waveyhang

Ruby Rock

Coverhang

Pyramid

Stonehenge Area

Crystal Boulder

drainage

Hobbit Area

Tension wire

Porpoise

Highball Wall

Manaray Boulder

Whale Block

Mushroom

Green Bear Trail

Bear Creek

Bear Peak West Ridge Trail

THE TRAIL ROCKS

These are located north of the Balarney Stones, main fall line, along the trail leading up and close to the Summit of Green Mountain's West Ridge.

EAST AND WEST BLOBS

These boulders are along the trail leading to the summit of Green Mountain's West Ridge. Steep problems exist on their north and west faces. The west sides are more slabby while the north faces are slightly overhung.

EAST BLOB

1. **North Ace V4 (B1)** Climb up the far-left side of the north face.
2. **North Case V7** On the far-right side of the north face, start with an undercling and edge in the overhang and reach for the better edges.

SACRED CLIFFS NORTHERN SPINE—TRAIL ROCKS

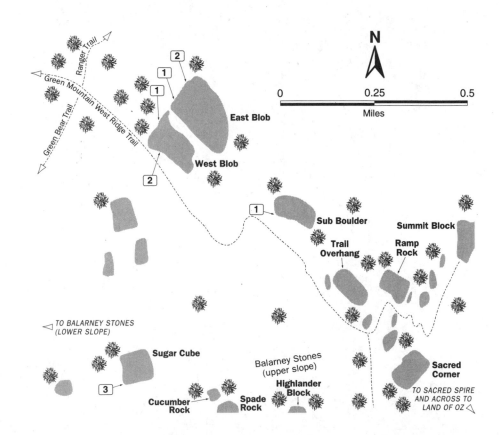

East and West Blobs   Sub Boulder

WEST BLOB

1. Crystal Left V3 Climb up the far-left side of the north face and mantel.

2. West Arête V2 Climb up the west face utilizing the arête to the slab.

SUB BOULDER

A few feet uptrail from the Blobs, you encounter this boulder on the northeast side of the trail. Good moderate problems are to be found.

1. The Nose V0 Climb up the west nose of the boulder.

2. Center South V0 Climb up the center of the south face via crystals.

RAMP ROCK

Continue uptrail from the Blob Boulders, past the Sub Boulder, and an overhanging trail rock to the steeper switchbacks, where you encounter the Ramp Rock sitting along the east side of the trail straight in front of you. Fun slab routes are found on its west face. From this rock, head straight off to the south to access the main Balarney Stones fall line.

1. West Slab V0 Climb up the center of the slab.

BALARNEY STONES

This array of boulders and blocks is amazing. You may hardly believe what you are seeing within this bouldered slope. From a point just below the summit of the Green Mountain West Ridge Trail, locate Ramp Rock and continue up off the main trail directly to the south for about 100 feet until you see the Sacred Corner. This is the

Ramp Rock

first of the Balarney Stones. From this corner, you begin to see more and more boulders down the slope to the west through the trees. The boulder slope extends all the way to the bottom (west) eventually intersecting with the Green Bear Trail. After the Sacred Corner, you encounter the Highlander Block, followed by the Cucumber and Spade Rocks. Below this, you find the Sugar Cube, a nice cube-shaped boulder. From the Sugar Cube, keep descending the fall line until you see the Power Boulder (an oval-shaped rock with a sheer south face) and the Butter Maroon (a large boulder with steep north, west and south faces). Immediately below this is the crystal-lined, overhanging Walrus Block. Farther down the slope about 100 yards you will come across the Balarney Spire and the Balarney Stone. These two latter rocks are something to see and offer unique challenges with great landings, as all the Balarney Stones do.

BALARNEY STONES (UPPER SLOPE)

THE SACRED CORNER
From Ramp Rock, head due south off the main trail and, in approximately 100 feet, you run into these great bouldering walls.

NORTH WALL
This makes up the northern side of the corner, forming a slot between the two walls.

    1. Suspicion V2 Climb up the left side of the south face.

    2. Riff-Raff V3 Climb the face right of the *Suspicion*.

    3. Love Triangles V0 Climb the pinchy groove up the middle of the face.

    4. Sinister V2 Climb the right side of the south face, utilizing the arête.

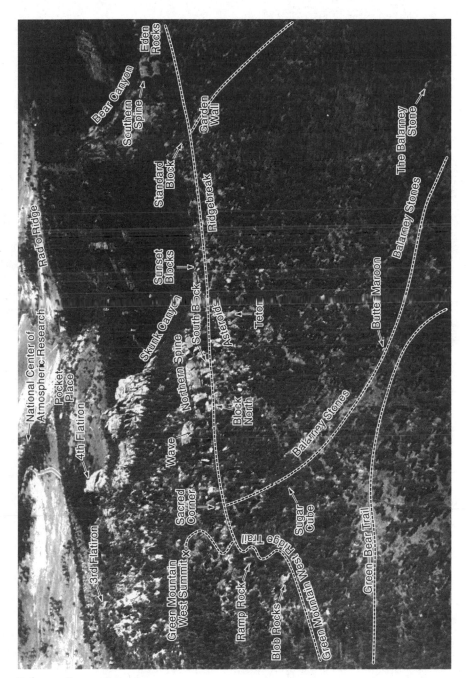

Balarney Stones Overview

Sacred Corner, north and south walls

SOUTH WALL

This rock makes up the south side of the corner.

1. **Karen's Crack V0** Layback the crack in the corner of the slot.

2. **Pathological Arête V0** Climb out of the slot, up and right to the arête.

3. **Cola V0** Climb the left side of the west face via large crystals.

4. **Peppy Slab V3** Climb up the center of the west face.

5. **Addictive V3** Climb the right side of the west face via a scoop.

6. **Princess of Darkness V3** Climb the south face just right of the arête.

7. **Three Strikes V0** Climb up the center of the south face.

Highlander Block   *The Sugar Cube*

THE HIGHLANDER BLOCK

This cubical boulder is about 20 feet below the Sacred Corner.

    1. The Highlander V2 Follow the left-facing corners on the left side.

    2. Highlander Arête V3 (hb) Climb the arête on the far-right side.

CUCUMBER ROCK (NOT PICTURED)

Just below the *Highlander Block* there is a cluster of boulders. Cucumber Rock is a pickle-shaped spire to the left and is the northernmost of the lot.

    1. Squash Wall V0 Climb up the middle of the west face.

SPADE ROCK (NOT PICTURED)

This is to the right, of Cucumber Rock and is the southernmost of the lot.

    1. NOAA Movers V7 Climb the arête on the far-left side of the west face.

THE SUGAR CUBE

This awesome boulder is found down in the trees about 60 yards below the Highlander Block. It offers great problems with good landings and is the first of the surprises that lie ahead. Descend its summit from the east.

    1. Saintly One V5 (hb) Climb up the middle of the west face.

    2. Middleman V4 (hb) Ascend the west face to the left of the crack.

    3. The Flying Overhang V3 (B1) (hb) Follows the crack to the top.

    4. Mat Mover V2 Climb the far-right side of the south face.

Note: To reach the following two boulders, hike downslope from the junction where

Bob Horan on the Highlander Arête *(V3), Highlander Block.*

James Palmer boulders up the Flying Overhang *(V3) on the Sugar Cube.*

the Green Mountain West Ridge Trail intersects the Ranger and Green Bear Trails. Head down the Green Bear Trail for a short ways to where it levels out in a nice forested section. The boulders sit just off to the left (south) side.

POWER BOULDER

This difficult, oval shaped boulder is located directly downslope approximately 30 yards from the Sugar Cube and is hidden somewhat in the trees. It sits just above and to the north of the larger Butter Maroon Boulder.

1. **Power Ranger V0** Climb the edges on the far-left side of the boulder.

2. **Power Flakes V3** Pull onto the face and reach up to the flakes.

3. **Power Step V3 (hb)** Step right onto the face then up the steep slab.

4. **Power On V4** Climb up the left side of the west face.

5. **Tales of Power V12?** The center of west face via slopey side-pulls.

6. **Power Mac V4** Climb the face via small edges left of the crack.

7. **Power Off V1** Climb the crack on the far-right side of the west face.

Power Boulder

Butter Maroon Boulder

BUTTER MAROON BOULDER

This large boulder is located immediately to the southwest of the Power Boulder. Many good highball problems exist. Descend to the east.

1. **Land O'Boulders V5 (hb)** Climb the far-left side of the northwest face, starting off small edges in the overhang and eventually reaching larger holds at the top.

2. **Peregrine V6–V7 (hb)** Climb the overhanging face left of the arête joining the crack.

3. **Sweet Arête V4 (hb)** Climb the arête to the crack above.

4. **Buffalo Gold V4 (B1) (hb)** Climb the layaway crack to the holds above.

5. **Parkay V5 (hb)** Climb the steep south face to the right of the layaway crack.

6. **Butter Rum V3** Climb the far-right side of south face.

Walrus Block

The author on Buffalo Gold *(V4), Butter Maroon Boulder.*

WALRUS BLOCK

Look for this block immediately downslope from the Butter Maroon. Walrus Block is located approximately halfway downslope from the upper summit trailway and offers a refreshing meadow-like hangout. Difficult pebble pinching exists on its west face. A few problems have been accomplished.

1. **CooCooCachu V0** Climb the slabby left side of the block.
2. **Textpert V4** Climb the left side of the block right of the slab problem.
3. **The Walrus V10?** Climb the overhanging west face of the block via small crystals.

BALARNEY STONES (LOWER SLOPE)

THE BALARNEY SPIRE

This is a prominent, pointy-topped rock set kindly on soft ground. It is found downslope from the Walrus Block, approximately 100 yards. Good problems exist across its north face. A few very enjoyable highballs exist on the left side. Exit to the south.

1. **Clover V0 (hb)** Climb the far-left side of the north face via the large pockets.
2. **Spireman V3 (hb)** Climb up the center of the north face to the very point at the top.

Balarney Spire and Balarney Stone

The Balarney Stone

3. **Four Leaf Clover V3** Climb the face via edges just right of *Spireman*. Exit right off shelf.

4. **Irishman V4** Climb the thin north face just left of the tree.

5. **Lucky V3** Climb the north face behind the tree via nice edges.

6. **Shamrock V2** Climb the north face right of the tree line.

THE BALARNEY STONE

This is a favorite big block within the Flatiron Range, comparable with Square Rock on Dinosaur Mountain. It is located immediately right of the spire. Descend to the south.

1. **End Game V4 (hb)** Climb the arête on far-left side of the east face, left of the dihedral.

2. **Dihedral Man V3 (hb)** Climb the dihedral on the left side of the east face.

3. **The Leprechaun V? (hb)** Climb the water mark up the center of the east face.

4. **Northern Lights V2 (hb)** Climb the arête on the northeast corner.

5. **North Face V4** Climb the north face via crystals just right of the arête.

6. **Big Dipper V2** Climbs northface via pods and crystals.

7. **Falling to Earth V2** Climb the north face just right of problems mentioned above.

8. **Balarney V3** Climb up the face on the right side via small edges.

9. **No Balarney V0** Climb the far-right side of the north face.

Note: There is good traversing on this block, as well as many easier highball slab problems found on the west side.

LAND OF OZ

This area consists of all the boulders and blocks between and below the Sacred Spire, Sacred Block North, and the Sacred Block South. From very near the summit of the Green Mountain West Ridge Trail, locate Ramp Rock and head off to the south staying close to the top of the ridge, continue past the Sacred Corner, located at the top of the Balarney Stones. A faint trail makes its way across to this area, where you first encounter the Sacred Spire. A wide variety of problems exist on the many rocks found within this secluded boulder pack.

NOTE: This area is off limits during nesting season, which begins on February 1st and lasts through July 31st. Find alternate destinations at this time.

SACRED SPIRE

This pointy rock is first encountered when hiking south along and below the summit ridge from the main trail. Continue past the Sacred Corner, directly to the south, to find this spire. A thin finger crack splits its west overhang. The spire sits on a shelf with other boulders below. Descend off this rock to the east by traversing the arête on the ridge.

1. **Space Shuttle V3 (hb)** Begin with the crack and heel hook over onto the southwest slab. Continue up the slab to the arête and follow it up and off the east side.

2. **Rockman V3** Climb up the overhang and arête on the left side of the west face.

Note: The south side of the spire offers fun slab problems. Also below the Sacred Spire are several other problems on isolated boulders, including a great traverse rock.

THE WAVE BLOCK

From the Sacred Spire, hike a short ways up and to the southeast, up a ramp, and continue along the summit blocks of the northern spine. This large block has an incredible overhanging west face with individual pocket routes leading up to a slab approximately 10 to 12 feet above. The crux of these routes is psychological when turning the lip. Pad and spotter recommended. Descend through the chimney on the north end.

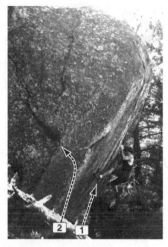

Sacred Spire

The Wave Block

1. **Hang Ten V4 (hb)** The pocketed face on the left side of the block, right of the crack.
2. **Surfs Up V5** Climb out overhang via pockets, just right of *Hang Ten*.
3. **Pocket Man V2 (B1-)** Climb out the center of the block via a layaway pocket reach.
4. **Under Tow V3** Start with good finger edges and reach for pockets right of *Pocket Man*.
5. **The Tube V3** Unless you are tall enough, climb in from the pockets on the right, out and left.

THE THUMB ROCK

This fun, challenging rock is located immediately south of the Wave.

1. **Watermelon Arête V2** Climb the north face via the arête.
2. **Watermelon Reach V3** Start on good holds and reach up to sloper with your left.
3. **Watermelon Face V0** Climb the right side of the west face via the big huecos.

Thumb Rock

Sugarplum Boulder

The Spearhead

SACRED BLOCK NORTH

This large multicolored block is visible just below the summit ridge to the southwest of the Wave Block. It forms an obstacle at a point where you must descend down and around in order to continue along the ridgetop heading south. It serves as a good landmark for locating the bouldering areas.

SUGARPLUM BOULDER

This boulder is located within the trees, below the Sacred Block North. The east face is steep, while the south face is slabby.

    1. Sugarplum Arête V2 Climb the arête on the northwest face.

    2. Sugarplum Slab V3 Climb the groove, slightly left of the middle of the south face.

SACRED BLOCK SOUTH (TETON AREA)

Continuing directly to the south from the Sacred Block North, you run into this beautifully colored, yellow-brown maroonish block just below the summit ridge. A steep, thin-edged, bolted route is apparent on its west face. Below this most prominent of northern spine blocks is an incredible spread of great boulders and problems beginning with the Asteroids and eventually leading to the Helix Block, Corridor Boulder, and Teton, followed downslope by the Wall Block to the northwest and the Play-Station to the southwest.

THE SPEARHEAD

Immediately west, below the Sacred Block South is this fine southwest-facing crystalled wall.

Middle Asteroid

North Asteroid

1. Spear West V0 Climb the left side of the southwest face via crystals.

THE ASTEROID BLOCKS

Just below the Sacred Block South, immediately below the Spearhead, there are four boulders with excellent moderate to difficult problems around them. Escape the summits to the east.

NORTH ASTEROID

This is the northernmost block, immediately south of the Spearhead.

1. Day in Life V0 Climb up the middle of the southwest face.

MIDDLE ASTEROID

This is the middle block, immediately southwest of the latter.

1. Comet Crack V3 (B1) Climb the crack on the left side of the west face.

2. Gnarly Tree V7 Ascend the face, right of center, via a crystal reach.

Note: Excellent slab problems from V0 to V3 are on the north face.

WEST ASTEROID

This block is located immediately west of the Middle Asteroid.

1. West One V1 Climb up the middle of the west face.

SKI SLAB (NOT PICTURED)

Look immediately north of the West Asteroid to find this block with its excellent V0 to V2 slab.

Pete Zoller sends the Comet Crack *(V3) on the Middle Asteroid.*

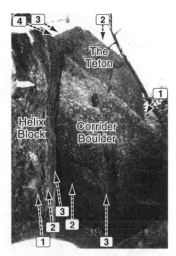

South Asteroid

Helix Block, Corridor Boulder, The Teton

SOUTH ASTEROID

This is located up and to the southeast of the Middle Asteroid. A dead tree lies on top.

1. **Tree Wall V2** Climb the flake and edge system up to the top.
2. **Mother's Helper V2** Climb the pockets on the right side of the wall.

HELIX BLOCK

This block is setting immediately west of the West Asteroid with a great place to hang out on top when bouldering in the Teton Area.

1. **Double Helix V3 (hb)** Climb up the far-left side of the west face.
2. **Dragon Wall V5 (hb)** Climb up the center of the west face.
3. **Stargate V3 (hb)** Climb up the far-right side of the west face.

CORRIDOR BOULDER

Immediately south of the Helix Block is this boulder forming the south corner of the cove. Problems are found on the east and north sides. The Teton is immediately south of this boulder.

1. **Center One V0** Climb the center of east face via good but small edges.
2. **Pixie Stick V7** Climb the far-left arête on the north face.
3. **Crystal Groove V4 (B1) (hb)** Climb up the crystalled groove on the north face.

Phyllis Fahey bouldering up the West One (V1) *on West Asteroid.*

The Teton

Cocoon Rock

THE TETON

This prominent Teton-shaped rock rises out above the scattered boulders and offers a great landmark from which one can access other boulders. It is found immediately south of the Asteroids, (below the Sacred Block South). The east side of the rock is the most practical way up, although problems have been seen on its south and west faces.

1. **Mangy Moose V3 (hb)** Climb the sheer face on the far-right, side of the west face, exit to the right short of the summit.

2. **Grande V2 (hb)** Climb up the center of the southeast face via crystals.

3. **Tits Ville V0 (hb)** Climb the crack line on the middle of the east face.

4. **The Hostel V4 (hb)** Climb the arête on the northeast corner.

COCOON ROCK

This rock is found due southeast of the Asteroid Boulders, up and right, southeast from the Teton.

1. **The Cocoon V3** Climb the middle of the north face via good crystals.

2. **Cooko Cocoon V2** Climb the northwest corner of the rock via edges.

3. **Gutterfly V0** Climb the face immediately right of the *Cooko Cocoon*.

THE WALL BLOCK

This block is located within the trees, approximately 30 yards slightly northwest, below the Teton. A larger rock forming a caved slot sits immediately to the west and also has a few fun and challenging problems.

1. **The Mist V6–V7 (hb)** Climb up the center of west face.

2. **Boreal V4** Climb the thin west face just right of *The Mist*.

The Play-Station Boulder

The Wall Block

3. **Ledge Walker V1** Climb the flake and ledge system on the right side of the west face.

BIG TIME BOULDER (NOT PICTURED)

This large boulder is located immediately below and almost touching the Wall Block. It has a nice caved slot with a few good problems as well as a steep west face. Good place to cool off in the heat of summer.

THE PLAY-STATION BOULDER

This boulder is located approximately 50 yards down, diagonally right, and southwest from the Teton.

1. **Remote Control V3** Climb the middle of the west face.

Sunset Cube   *Sunset Spike*

SUNSET BLOCKS

On the far-right (south) summit of the northern spine, the cliff thins out into short blocks and outcrops. These beautifully boulderable formations are well worth the visit and a great place to have a ridgetop picnic or sunset bouldering session. Some of the rock shapes are reminiscent of those on Flagstaff Mountain, although the rock is a bit smoother.

SUNSET CUBE

Before reaching the end of the northern spine, you see this blackened cube. The north face has a hanging start onto its steep face.

1. Black Ice V6–V7 Pull onto the north face via small crimpy crystals.

2. Blackened Arête V4 Climb the leaning arête on the northwest edge.

SUNSET SPIKE

This pinnacle is located on the far-right summit ridge just before its tail end. Hike due south from the Sunset Cube for about 50 yards.

1. Southside Jahosa V0 Climb the south face of the pinnacle.

SPIKE BLOCK

Just right, almost attached to *Sunset Spike* is this block.

2. North Wall V2 Climb up the north face via vertical slab work.

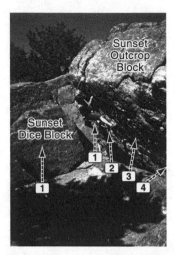

Sunset Outcrop, Sunset Dice Blocks

SUNSET OUTCROP BLOCK

This ridgetop outcrop makes up the very far-right, southern end of the Sacred Cliff's Northern Spine. Many good problems are found on its overhanging west face. Hike south along the ridge, past an outcrop with highball cracks.

1. Arêtes Away V2 Climb the arête on the far-left side of the outcrop.

2. Cracking Up V2 Climb the overhanging crack on the left side.

3. Crystal Dyno V7–V8 Utilize the large crystal in the center of the face.

4. Sunscreen V1 Climb up the right side of the outcrop, left of the block.

SUNSET DICE BLOCK

Sunset Dice is to your left when you face Sunset Outcrop.

1. Nice and Easy V0 Climb up the south face of the block.

RIDGEBREAK BOULDERS

These boulders are found directly below and slightly right of the Sunset Summit Blocks, where the summit ridge becomes a rockless saddle. Excellent bouldering is offered on boulders unique to this particular ridge zone. Head downslope to discover several good rocks.

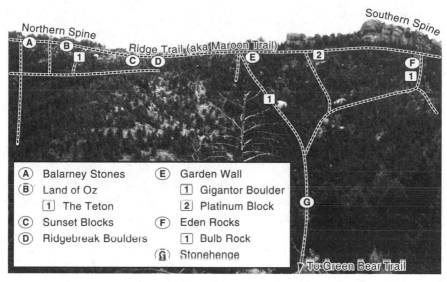

A Balarney Stones
B Land of Oz
   1 The Teton
C Sunset Blocks
D Ridgebreak Boulders

E Garden Wall
   1 Gigantor Boulder
   2 Platinum Block
F Eden Rocks
   1 Bulb Rock
G Stonehenge

Ridgebreak Overview

RIDGEBREAK BOULDER

This is an awesome boulder offering a wide variety of unique challenges. It is the first of the boulders encountered while descending from the ridge top.

1. **Hanging Arête V6** Climb the hanging northwestern arête.
2. **Leaning Crack V5** This unique leaning crack offers a great challenge.
3. **Pod Reach V3** From the large hueco on the west face, gain the top.
4. **Right One V0** Climb the slab on the right side of the boulder.

Ridgebreak Boulder

Interceptor Boulder

INTERCEPTOR BOULDER

This boulder is located down in the trees a short distance from the Ridgebreak Boulder. Fun face problems in the V0 range can be found on its west face.

1. **Interceptor V0** Climb the west face just right of the tree.
2. **Intersection V0** Climb the west face just right of the *Interceptor*.
3. **Inner Course V0** Climb the west face left of the southwestern nose.

SACRED CLIFFS—SOUTHERN SPINE

This portion of the Sacred Cliffs is characterized by well-endowed fall lines of boulders situated below the large spire-like formations. The descending boulders are scattered throughout the trees and are most easily reached by traversing from the Northern Spine Ridge Trail, following it to the south. The first blocks and boulders encountered, on the far-left northernmost portion of the Southern Spine, are the Garden Walls, Standard Block, Thanksgiving Boulder, Druid Spire, Mime Maroon, Carmel Block, Robert's Rock, Gigantor Boulder, and the Platinum Block. Farther south along the summit you find, just below the ridgetop, the Eden Rocks, consisting of the Bulb Rock, Jung's Block and Boulder, Hobbit Block, the Arrowhead, Coin Rock, and the Serpent Block.

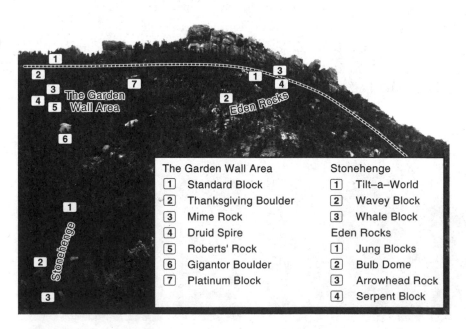

The Garden Wall Area		Stonehenge	
1	Standard Block	1	Tilt–a–World
2	Thanksgiving Boulder	2	Wavey Block
3	Mime Rock	3	Whale Block
4	Druid Spire	Eden Rocks	
5	Roberts' Rock	1	Jung Blocks
6	Gigantor Boulder	2	Bulb Dome
7	Platinum Block	3	Arrowhead Rock
		4	Serpent Block

Southern Spine Overview

GARDEN WALL AREA

This array of boulders and blocks is found at the far-northern summit of the Sacred Cliff's Southern Spine. Hike to a point just below the first large formations of the spine. The first block you see is the Standard Block. This awesome block is hard to miss, for its cubical shape with good landings is one you might dream about. Just below, you cross the Thanksgiving Boulder. Its steep south face is covered with crystals and edges. Farther below and to the north you find the Druid Spire. Directly across to the southeast you reach the Mime Maroon, consisting of extremely thin and steep face routes up its west side. Just up and right is the Carmel Block, with a fun, semi-highball center route up its west overhang. Below the Mime and slightly right you will eventually run into Robert's Rock, with an overhanging west face and very challenging problems. Below this is the Gigantor Boulder which has awesome problems on its south side, as well as a classic trad overhang on its west face. The Platinum Block is located across the slope to the south approximately 75 yards from the Carmel Block. Its west face is hidden within the trees and offers great overhanging problems.

THE STANDARD BLOCK

This block is visible from the summit ridge trail at the beginning of the Southern Spine's north end. The blocks don't get much better than this. Descend from the large crystalled east face.

1. **Wavey V2** Climb the left side of south face.
2. **The Groove V3** Climb the south face via pockets and an undercling right of *Wavey*.
3. **Stylin' V3** Climb up the laybacks and edges just right of *The Groove*.
4. **Standard Shield V2 (B1-)** Climb the varnished shield via layaway pockets.
5. **Crystalled Scoop V4** Climb the obvious crystal-lined scoop of the southeast corner.
6. **Crystal Arête V0** Climb up crystals right of the *Crystalled Scoop*.
7. **Short Crystal V0** Climb up crystals on the center of the east face.

The Standard Block

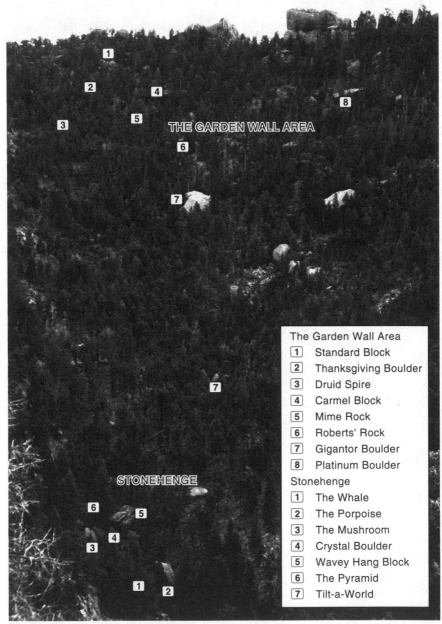

The Garden Wall Area
1 Standard Block
2 Thanksgiving Boulder
3 Druid Spire
4 Carmel Block
5 Mime Rock
6 Roberts' Rock
7 Gigantor Boulder
8 Platinum Boulder

Stonehenge
1 The Whale
2 The Porpoise
3 The Mushroom
4 Crystal Boulder
5 Wavey Hang Block
6 The Pyramid
7 Tilt-a-World

Garden Wall and Stonehenge Overview

Thanksgiving Boulder

THANKSGIVING BOULDER

This boulder is located immediately downslope to the north from the Standard Block. Many challenging and somewhat thin problems utilizing crystals and small edges have been established.

1. **Mashed Potatoes V5** Climb the southwestern nose of the south face.

2. **Turkey Bird V6** Climb the south face, right of *Mashed Potatoes*, utilizing underclings and crystals.

3. **Gravy V4** Climb up the center of the south face via pockets and crystals.

4. **Stuffing V1** Climb the right side of the south face via good holds.

Eric Johnson works for the Gravy *(V4) on Thanksgiving Boulder.*

Rob Hart bouldering up the awesome Groove (V3) *on the south face of the Standard Block, Garden Wall Area.*

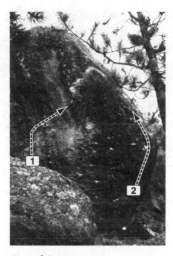

Druid Spire

Mime Maroon

DRUID SPIRE

From the Thanksgiving Boulder, head straight down into the trees for about 50 yards until you run into this spire.

1. **Superstition V4 (hb)** Climb the overhanging north face, up and out right.

2. **Druid Tune V2 (hb)** Climb the west arête starting with a large crystal for your left.

MIME MAROON

From the Thanksgiving Boulder, descend down and left (south) for a short ways until you find this fine piece of maroon. The west face offers very steep and difficult face problems.

1. **The Mime V6 (hb)** Climb the thin west face on the left side.

2. **Mime's Arête V5 (hb)** Climb the face and arête on the right side.

Carmel Block

Robert's Rock

CARMEL BLOCK

This block is up and slightly right from the Mime Maroon. It has a carmel-colored tint to it and an overhanging west face with a bucket flake system.

1. **Carmel Cone V3 (hb)** Climb out the center of the west face.

Note: Many good face problems on the south face also exist. The routes range from V0 to V4.

ROBERT'S ROCK

This rock is downhill to the southwest from the Mime Rock. It has an overhanging west face with several good hard problems.

1. **Crystal Ball V6** Start with the crystal on the far-left side of the west face.

2. **Crimpy Cling V5** Climb the layaway undercling on the far-right side of the west face.

3. **Crystal Pinch Overhang V8** From the crystal just above the undercling, reach the top.

GIGANTOR BOULDER

Down below Mine Maroon and Roberts Rock, you eventually run into a giant boulder with an extremely overhanging west face, somewhat more like a roof. The flake system out the west side of this roof goes at 5.12, lead in traditional style by Bob Horan, then bouldered out. On the south side of this huge overhang, there is a problem that offers good holds up the steep bulging wall. Exit to the east. This is perhaps the largest boulder in the Maroon Garden.

Note: From this boulder you can descend down towards the bottom of the gully, towards the Green Bear Trail, to reach the Stonehenge Area.

1. **Tobar V7 (hb)** Climb the steep, overhanging, bulging south wall of the boulder.

2. **The Surf V7** Climb up the left side of the south face, out the bulges.

Gigantor Boulder

PLATINUM BLOCK

This awesome block has a severely overhanging west face hidden in the trees. It offers some of the best overhanging bouldering in the garden. It is located across the gully to the south from the heart of the Garden Wall Area, sitting downslope below the summit ridge. Exit its east side.

1. Plato's Arête V6 Climb up the arête on the far-left side.

Platinum Block

Matt Samet cranks the desperate reach move of the Main Hang *(V5) on the Platinum Block.*

2. **Socrate's Overhang V5 (B1+)** Climb up the wall right of *Plato's Arête*, starting down low.

3. **Pop Overhangs V2** Several variations are possible out this midsection.

4. **Main Hang V5** Climb out the overhang, right of *Pops Overhangs*, starting right and reaching out to the left. A difficult large crystal pinch is utilized at the lip.

5. **Platinum Overhang V8** Climb the big overhang right of the latter.

6. **Platinum Traverse V12?** Traverse from the right to the left.

EDEN ROCKS

This spread of blocks and boulders is found at the highpoint on the south end of the southern spine just before it descends down into the far-west end of Bear Canyon. The boulders and blocks here begin a southwestern fall line of rock that eventually works its way down, intersecting the Green Bear Trail below. Many rocks appear along this fall line but the cream of the crop sits high up on the summit ridge. Its lower portion, close to the Green Bear Trail, is the Hobbit Area. From the high point of the southern spine, descend down to the northwest until you come across a nice meadow break with a cluster of good quality boulders sitting just north of the ridge crest. The first boulder encountered on the east side of the cluster is the Sheer Maroon followed by the Bulb Rock to the north and the Hobnail Boulder to the south.

Down to Green Bear Trail

Sacred Cliffs Southern Spine

Eden Rocks

To Bulb Dome

Upper Hobbit Slope

To Lower Hobbit Slopes

Eden Rocks
1 Jung's Block
2 Hobbit Block
3 Serpent Block
4 Arrowhead Rock
5 Coin Rock

Upper Hobbit Slope
6 Corridor Rocks
7 The Big Blocks
8 Quartz Buttress

Southern Spine Overview

Sheer Maroon *Bulb Rock, west face*

SHEER MAROON

This sheer rock has a thin vertical west-facing slab. A few good face problems have been done.

    1. Sheer West V0 Climb the left side of the west face.

BULB ROCK

Immediately north of the Sheer Maroon, and somewhat attached, you find this large, problem-endowed, dome-shaped rock. Traversing is also an option. Exit to the east.

    1. Lantern V6 Climb up the thin face on the far-left side of the west face.

    2. Cervazi General V2 Climb layback seam to the right of *Lantern*.

    3. Western Flake V2 (hb) Climb the flake route in the center of the face.

    4. Western Electric V6–V7 Climb the sheer micro slab, on the right side.

    5. Slabs Away V3 Climb the thin slab to the left of the crack.

    6. Southern Crack V1 Climb the crack line on the south face.

    7. Slabbo V4 Climb the slab on the right side of the crack.

HOBNAIL BOULDER

Located immediately to the south of the Bulb Rock.

    1. Crystals Away V0 Climb up the center of the west face.

JUNG'S BLOCK

From the Bulb Rock, head due south for approximately 100 feet and you run into these fine rocks. From up top, once you reach the ridgecrest of the Sacred Cliff's Southern Spine, at a point where you can see down south into the far-west end of

Bulb Rock and Hobnail Boulder

Jung's Block and Jung's Boulder

Mike Mead on the steep Analysand *(V6) on the Jung's Boulder.*

Hobbit Block

Jung's Boulder

Bear Canyon, descend the meadowed slope to the southwest. The Jung's Block and Boulder are sitting on the crest below. They are somewhat hard to see when approaching from the north. The bouldering is found in a southeast-facing cove formed by the two blocks. Jung's Block is the more southwestern of the two.

1. **South Overhanger V6 (hb)** On the south face of the block there is a steep, somewhat overhanging face with good holds.

2. **Pocket Arête V3** Climb to the top via pockets on the southeast arête.

3. **Crystal's Wall V0–V2** This is the first of a series of short, fun problems starting on the far-left (south) end of the block, moving then to the right (north) end of the block. Pick and choose a variation.

JUNG'S BOULDER

This is the perfectly steep and varied boulder on the north end of the alcove. A few very difficult problems are found on the south face.

1. **Animus V5** Climb the west face of the block via small crystals and edges.

2. **Analysand V6** Climb the southwest arête.

3. **Anima V8 (B2)** Climb the steep, south-facing corner utilizing the thin seam.

HOBBIT BLOCK

This block is located down to the south of the Jung's Block and Boulder and offers fun, steep problems on its south and west faces.

1. **Holy Hobbit V0** Climb the left side of the west face.

2. **Hobbit Habit V4 (B1)** Climb the right side of the west face, left of the arête.

3. **Tolkien's Face V4** Climb the left side of the south face.

Arrowhead Rock

The Coin

4. Rings of Fire V1 Climb up the center of the south face.

5. Very Nice V0 Climb the right side of the south face.

ARROWHEAD ROCK

This interesting rock resembles a giant arrowhead and is located up against and below the tall overhanging summit block formation of the southern spine. From Jung's Block, head uphill and slightly south until up against the summit towers. The rock is shaped like a giant arrowhead and offers a few excellent face problems. A spotter and crash pad are very helpful.

1. Crazyhorse V5 (B1+) This problem climbs up the middle of the south face.

THE COIN

This circular rock is located immediately south, across from the Arrowhead and connected to the main formation.

1. Coin Toss V1 (hb) Climb the north face of the rock starting on its right side and then up and left.

Serpent Block

SERPENT BLOCK

Just below the Coin to the northwest, down and somewhat hidden amidst the brush, is this entrancing block, which offers daring problems up its south face. Its north face also offers steep face problems with a more reasonable landing. Exit to the east.

1. **Apple's Way V4 (hb)** Climb the short corner line on the left side of the south face.

2. **Original Line V3 (hb)** Climb the center of the south face via good edges. Starts from the right side.

3. **Northern Son V3** Climb up the middle of the north face via small edges.

STONEHENGE

From the junction where the Green Mountain West Ridge Trail meets the Green Bear Trail, hike down to the bottom of the Green Bear Trail, eventually heading due south. Just past the junction of the Bear Peak Trail and Green Bear Trail, the trail begins to rise a bit and then goes under the tension wires. Once at the top of the knoll, almost directly below the tension wires, head out to the east, skirting around to the south-east on the northern slope above the gully. Once around the short ridgebreak, look down into the gully to see the first Stonehenge rocks.

WHALE BLOCK

This is the first maroon block you see when descending into and hiking up the gully to the east. Its sheer west face has challenging, short-but-sweet problems. Whale Block is the northernmost block of the two, making up the northwest facing alcove.

1. **The Spout V2** On the far-left, northern end, climb to top via a hole.

Whale Block and Porpoise Rock

2. Save the Whale V2 Climb the good set of edges to the top.

3. Monowhale V6 From a strenuous mono pull reach the top.

4. Right On V1 Climb up the far-right end of the block.

PORPOISE SPIRE

This rock is located immediately south of Whale Block and forms the southern end of the northwest-facing alcove. Good problems exist on its north face. Exit to the south.

1. Dolphin Free V4 (hb) From a strenuous undercling on the left end of the north face extend up to good edges with the left hand and then work up the layback system.

2. The Porpoise V5 (hb) From the undercling on the right, reach across to the left, then up.

3. No Porpoise V0 This is a great bucket haul up and over the right side of the rock.

MUSHROOM BOULDER

This magnificent boulder is found immediately up from Whale Block and Porpoise Spire and forms the northern wall of this southwest facing alcove. Difficult problems, including a classic traverse are to be found.

1. Huecoed Shroom V1 Climb the left side of the west face via pockets.

2. Crystaled One V2 Climb the center of the west face pulling on with a crystal and edge.

Mushroom Boulder

3. **Shroom's Arête V3** Climb the arête on the southwest corner.

4. **Magic Mushroom V4** Beginning on two crystals, reach up for the pocketed edge.

5. **Hooka V6** Layback and extend to the top, reaching the shallow pocket.

6. **The Mushroom V4** From the large undercling, reach up to the seam, then pocket.

7. **Mushroom Traverse V4–V6** Start on the right or left and traverse back and forth. Finish with *Magic Mushroom* or *The Mushroom* for added difficulty.

CRYSTAL BOULDER

This dome-shaped boulder is located immediately east, somewhat attached to the Mushroom Boulder.

1. **Crystal Crimper V7** Climb up the center of west face utilizing the small crystals.

THE WAVEY HANG BLOCK (NOT PICTURED)

This block is located directly behind the Crystal Boulder and offers a few fun problems. Its west side has a great overhanging cave-like roof, offering great shelter from the rain.

1. **Wavey Hang V2** On the northwest side of the block there is a slopey face.

The Pyramid Rock

Crystal Boulder

THE PYRAMID ROCK

Immediately behind the Wavey Hang Block there is this nice south-facing rock.

   1. **Tut V2** Climb the left side of the south face.

   2. **Oneeye V1** Climb up the right side.

TILT-A-WORLD BLOCK

From the Pyramid, hike a short ways uphill to the south and you run right into this challenging block.

   1. **Superduper V6** Starting from the big layback edge pull and reach up to the next ledge.

   2. **Grande Central V8** Climb up the center of east face using laybacks.

   3. **Superwoman V4** Climb up the right side of the east face.

HOBBIT AREA

This area is accessed in two ways. Hike up from the Bear Canyon Trail, past Bear Canyon to the west, past the Tree Shadow Area, until you reach the lower southern portion of the Sacred Cliff's Southern Spine, then continue up to the far west just before Stonehenge. The other way is from the Green Mountain West Ridge Trail. Take the Green Bear Trail downhill, past Stonehenge and around to the next ridge and fall line of rock. A block is visible on the east side of the trail just south of the gully line.

Tilt-a-World Block

Manaray Rock

HOBBIT TRAIL ROCKS

These boulders are found along the Bear Canyon Trail, approximately 100 yards west of the Sacred Cliff's Southern Spine leading to the heart of the Hobbit Area.

MANARAY ROCK

When approaching from Bear Canyon, continue hiking past the Sacred Cliff's Southern Spine, approximately 100 yards to the west, and you come across a meadowed area with an interesting little spire-like rock setting on the west side of the trail. It has a sheer north face.

    1. **Manaray Face V5** Climb up the center of the sheer north face.

SPUD ROCK

Across the trail to the east you can see this rock. It looks somewhat like a mini tail-end of a ridge.

    1. **The Spud V3** Climb up the left side of the south face.

Spud Rock

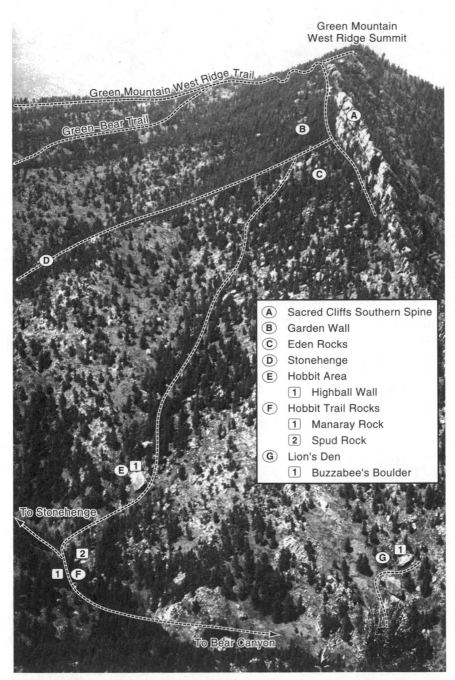

Green Mountain
West Ridge Summit

Green Mountain West Ridge Trail

Green-Bear Trail

Ⓐ Sacred Cliffs Southern Spine
Ⓑ Garden Wall
Ⓒ Eden Rocks
Ⓓ Stonehenge
Ⓔ Hobbit Area
  1 Highball Wall
Ⓕ Hobbit Trail Rocks
  1 Manaray Rock
  2 Spud Rock
Ⓖ Lion's Den
  1 Buzzabee's Boulder

To Stonehenge

To Bear Canyon

Southern Spine, Hobbit Area Overview

Highball Wall, south face

HIGHBALL WALL

Continue a short way uptrail to the north until you locate a block upslope to the right (east) side of the trail. This block has a steep west face. Up the gully and slope behind this is the large blocky boulder named Highball Wall.

1. **Tequila Face V1** Climb the far-left side of the south face.

2. **Martini Face V2** Climb just right of *Tequila Face* via a big crystal.

3. **Beer Thirty V3 (hb)** Climb the face right of *Martini Face*.

4. **Sunrise Face V5 (hb)** Climb up on the right side of the south face beginning at the roof.

5. **Ghetto Simulator V4** Traverse across the lip on the west side of the boulder.

Ghetto Simulator

Coverhang

Ruby Block

RUBY BLOCK

This cubical boulder is located upslope from Highball Wall. Scramble past several okay-looking boulders and rocks to a level spot in the trees.

    1. South Scoop V1 Climb up the south face via good holds.

    2. Gem Corner V3 Climb the southeast arête.

    3. Keepsake Ruby V2 Climb the east face via good holds.

COVERHANG

Continue upslope and slightly right, southeast from the Ruby, and you run into this large block with a huge south-facing overhang just off the ground.

    1. Coverhang Lip Traverse V6 Traverse the lip of the south overhang.

Buzzabee's Boulder

LION'S DEN

These boulders are found by hiking in from the east up the Bear Canyon Trail. Continue west on the Bear Canyon Trail, past the northern slopes of Bear Canyon's West Ridge, past the Sacred Cliff's Southern Spine, to the first gully coming off the slopes. A large, crystal-endowed boulder is visible the north from the trail. Head up and behind this large boulder.

BUZZABEE'S BOULDER

This boulder is found up to the east behind the large boulder seen from the trail. Head upslope to the northeast. The south face of this boulder has awesome face routes.

1. **Cigars V2** Climb the face on the far-left side of the boulder
2. **Doobee V5** Climb up the center of the south face via small edges.
3. **Microbrew V6** Climb up the steep, thin-edged face right of *Doobee*.
4. **Rioriffic V4** Climb the steep wall on the far-right side of the boulder.

THE FLATIRONS

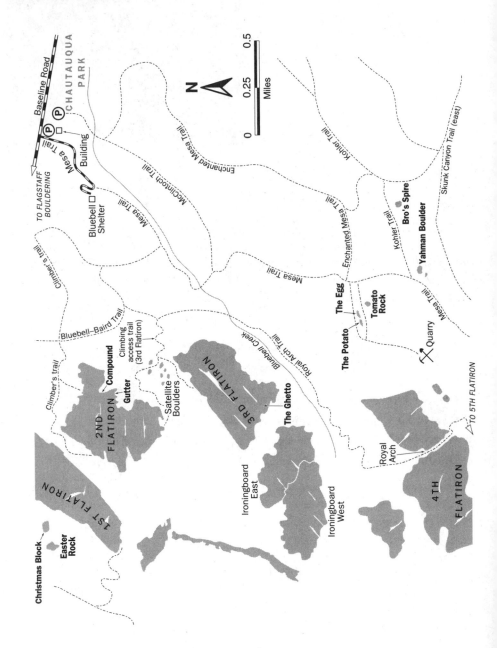

Baseline Road

TO FLAGSTAFF BOULDERING

CHAUTAUQUA PARK

P P

Building

Mesa Trail

Bluebell Shelter

Climber's trail

McClintock Trail

Enchanted Mesa Trail

Mesa Trail

N

Miles
0   0.25   0.5

Kohler Trail

Skunk Canyon Trail (east)

Enchanted Mesa Trail

Mesa Trail

Bro's Spire

Kohler Trail

Yahman Boulder

The Egg

Tomato Rock

The Potato

Quarry

Mesa Trail

Bluebell–Baird Trail

Climbing access trail (3rd Flatiron)

Climber's trail

Compound

Gutter

2ND FLATIRON

Satellite Boulders

Bluebell Creek

Royal Arch Trail

3RD FLATIRON

The Ghetto

Ironingboard East

Ironingboard West

Royal Arch

4TH FLATIRON

TO 5TH FLATIRON

1ST FLATIRON

Christmas Block

Easter Rock

THE FLATIRONS

BLUEBELL AREA

This area consists of problems within the Second Flatiron and Third Flatiron, as well as the isolated boulders on the southern slopes of Bluebell Canyon. Within these famous and picturesque Flatirons, you find amazing rock slots such as The Compound, The Gutter, and The Ghetto, as well as The Satellite Boulders. At the mouth of Bluebell Canyon, are the Tomato, the Egg, and the Potato. These boulders offer good, fun problems.

NOTE: The Third Flatiron is closed during raptor season and open from July 31st through February 1st (as of 1999). Check with park regulations, for this could change over the years. Stiff fines are enforced. Find alternate destinations while the closures are in effect.

Directions: Locate Baseline Road in Boulder and drive due west to Grant Street, located just before the foot of the mountains. Turn left into Chautauqua Park. Parking is obvious. Hike up from the ranger cottage, located at the south end of the parking lot, up the paved road. This takes you up to the Bluebell Shelter. To reach the Satellite Boulders, The Gutter, and The Compound, take the Bluebell-Baird Trail up from the shelter to the north until reaching the Third Flatiron Climbing Access Trail. Take this trail up to the west. The trail winds up to the northeast side of the Third Flatiron. At that point you begin to see the Satellite Boulders scattered along the trail. To reach the Gutter and the Compound, continue to the north through the Boulders until you see the base of the Second Flatiron. The Gutter is visible down and right of the massive overhang protruding from the east slab. The Compound is slightly up and behind The Gutter.

History: The boulder problems fashioned in this area are attributable to a handful of locals such as Jay Droeger at the Satellite Boulders; John Dunn and Paul Glover for much of the work at the Ghetto, Gutter, and Compound; and Bob Horan for Bluebell Canyon and beyond.

Northern Flatirons Overview

SECOND FLATIRON

THE GUTTER

This slot is located on the east side of the Second Flatiron below and slightly right (north) of the massive overhang protruding from its eastern slab. It offers an excellent overhanging roof problem that extends in an upper diagonaling manner in the slot.

    1. Gutter Traverse V7 Traverse up the slot starting down and right.

THE COMPOUND

This somewhat bulging, double-bouldered slot of maroon is on the east side of the Second Flatiron above and right of the Gutter. It offers excellent traversing as well as overhanging problems out its bulging walls. Pick and choose a route.

    1. Compound Traverse V6 Traverse the length of the two maroons.

The Gutter

The Compound

THIRD FLATIRON

THE SATELLITE BOULDERS (NOT PICTURED)

These boulders are along the trail leading up to the Third Flatiron. From Bluebell Shelter, follow signs leading up to the Third Flatiron's northside. These boulders offer a few good problems.

THE GHETTO

This awesome slot is on the western side of the Third Flatiron and is accessible via a west-side gully and short cliff leading to its secluded bench. Many excellent problems exiting its roofs exist, as well as the classic *Ghetto Traverse* which skirts the big jugs hanging from the slots lip.

Directions: From Chautauqua Park, head up the paved road to the Bluebell Shelter. Take the Royal Arch Trail, up through Bluebell Canyon, to a point past the west face of the Third Flatiron. At this point you must locate the gully leading up to the Third Flatiron's west face. Scan the west face for an elongated ledge system. A short face must be climbed to reach this shelf where The Ghetto is located (see Map).

THIRD FLATIRON/GHETTO AREA

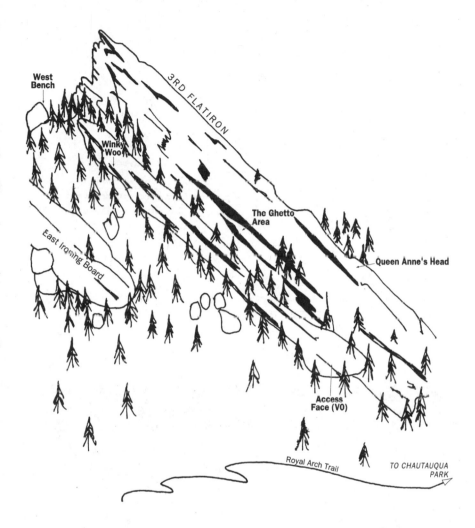

West
Bench

3RD FLATIRON

Winky
Woo

East Ironing Board

The Ghetto
Area

Queen Anne's Head

Access
Face (V0)

Royal Arch Trail

TO CHAUTAUQUA
PARK

GHETTO TRAVERSE ROCK

This rock is the northernmost of the two rocks that make up the Ghetto.

1. **Guanophobia V6** Climb the caved slot on the far-left side of the rock.
2. **Inner Space V4** Climb the holds out the roof just right of *Guanophobia*.
3. **Ghetto Traverse V3 (B1)** Traverse up the lip starting down low and right.

THIRD FLATIRON, SOUTHWEST FACE

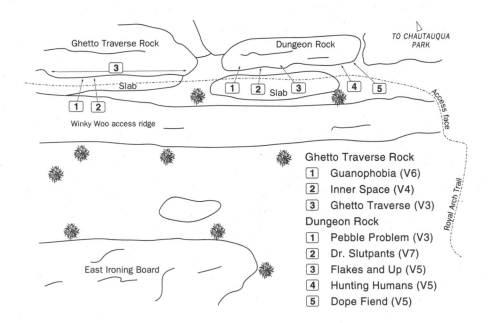

Ghetto Traverse Rock

Dungeon Rock

TO CHAUTAUQUA PARK

Slab

Winky Woo access ridge

East Ironing Board

Access face

Royal Arch Trail

Ghetto Traverse Rock
1. Guanophobia (V6)
2. Inner Space (V4)
3. Ghetto Traverse (V3)

Dungeon Rock
1. Pebble Problem (V3)
2. Dr. Slutpants (V7)
3. Flakes and Up (V5)
4. Hunting Humans (V5)
5. Dope Fiend (V5)

The Ghetto

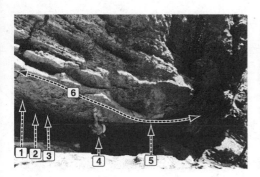

Dungeon Rock

The Tomato

DUNGEON ROCK

This rock is the southernmost rock of the Ghetto Area.

1. **Pebble Problem V3** Climb up the overhang utilizing the pebbles on the far-right side.

2. **Dr. Slut Pants V7** Climb the overhang right of the *Pebble Problem*.

3. **Flakes and Up V5** Climb the overhang right of *Dr. Slut Pants* utilizing the flake system.

4. **Hunting Humans V5** Starting down low, climb out the overhang located right of *Flakes and Up*.

5. **Dope Fiend V5** Climb the overhang on the far-right side of the rock.

6. **Anicostia Traverse V10** Traverse across the Dungeon Rock.

BLUEBELL CANYON

THE TOMATO

Take the Mesa Trail south (before the Bluebell Shelter), until you are just past the McClintoch Trail junction. Follow the thin trail heading up to the west and you soon run across this rock. Many fun, short problems surround this boulder.

THE EGG

This rock is found upslope and right from the Tomato, behind some old woodwork ruins and smaller boulders. A few difficult problems are found on its north face. A spotter is recommended.

1. **Scramble V4** Climb up the left side of the north face.

2. **Poached V7–V8** Climb up the severely overhanging right side.

The Egg   *The Potato*

THE POTATO

This small dome-shaped boulder is found immediately right (west) of the Egg. Challenging problems are found on its north face. Exit to the south.

1. **Left Spud V4** Climb up the left side of the bulge utilizing a stem.
2. **The Middle Spud V3** Reach up for the good holds right of *Left Spud*.
3. **The Potato V6** Climb directly up the right side of the north face.
4. **Right Spud V4** Climb up the far-right side of the north face.

ROYAL MEADOWS

The boulders found amidst these meadows are quite nice and offer a wide variety of classic challenges. All are located east of the Mesa Trail within the meadows of the Fourth and Fifth Flatirons and Skunk Canyon. Take the Mesa Trail from Chautauqua Park, past the Enchanted Mesa Trail junction up toward the Skunk Canyon Trail.

FOURTH AND FIFTH FLATIRONS (ROYAL MEADOWS)

YAHMAN BOULDER

This boulder is found immediately to the south of the junction where the Kohler Trail meets the Mesa Trail.

1. **Pink Floyds V4** Climb up the bulging south face of the boulder.
2. **Yahman Traverse V5** Starts either from the far-left or right and traverses back and forth along the crackline.

BRO'S ROCK

This mini-spire is located along the ridge to the east of the Yahman Boulder. Head along the ridge to the east for several hundred yards. The rock sits on the northern slopes of the canyon.

1. **Bro's Route V0** Climb up the middle of the south face.

FOURTH AND FIFTH FLATIRONS, ROYAL MEADOWS OVERVIEW

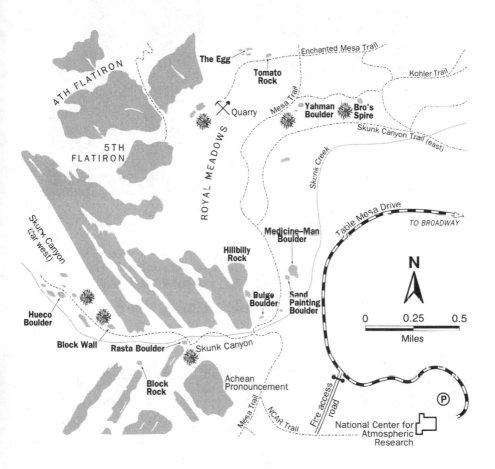

SKUNK CANYON

Skunk Canyon offers some very worthwhile boulders east and west of the main ridges of the inner canyon. Follow the creekbed from the east, up to and through the canyon, around to the north, and you come upon all of these boulders.

Directions: From the National Center for Atmospheric Research (NCAR) at the west end of Table Mesa Drive in Boulder, hike the NCAR Trail to the west, eventually intersecting the Mesa Trail. Head to the north, down past a gully, and then up to the

Yahman Boulder

Bro's Rock

heart of the canyon. Go to the east to access the Bulge Boulder, Roof Rock, and Medicine Man Boulder. Go to the west into the inner canyon and eventually through to the northwest for Rasta Boulder, Block Wall, and the Hueco Boulder.

NOTE: All ridges behind Ridge One are closed for nesting from February 1st to July 31st. Find alternate destinations during this time.

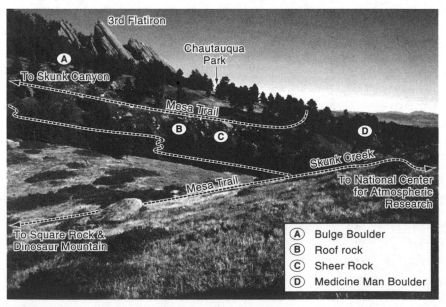

Skunk Canyon east

Bulge Boulder

Roof Rock

SKUNK CANYON—EAST

BULGE BOULDER

From NCAR, take the Mesa Trail north to the front of Skunk Canyon. This boulder is located on the northern slopes, east of the first ridges of Skunk Canyon.

1. Power Bulge V3 Climb up the middle of the southeast face.

ROOF ROCK

Continue to the east along the Mesa Trail and look down to the right (south) to see this roofed rock very near the trail.

1. South Roof V3 Climb up and out the south roof.

SAND PAINTING BOULDER

Continue east from the Roof Rock along the Mesa Trail until it turns to the north. After approximately 100 feet (hiking north), look down to the east to see the tops of these nice boulders. This boulder has challenging, steep face problems on its east face and is somewhat attached to the Medicine Man Boulder.

1. Sands of Time V3 Climb up the middle of the east face.

MEDICINE MAN BOULDER

This is one of the nicest boulders in the meadows east of Skunk Canyon. It is the large boulder down from and somewhat attached to the Sand Painting Boulder. Awesome overhanging problems with a very interesting little cave are found on its east side.

1. What's Up Doc V3 (hb) Climb up the left side of the boulder.

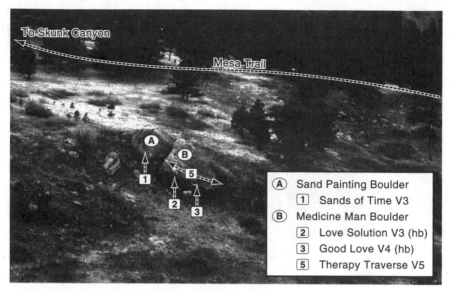

Ⓐ	Sand Painting Boulder
[1]	Sands of Time V3
Ⓑ	Medicine Man Boulder
[2]	Love Solution V3 (hb)
[3]	Good Love V4 (hb)
[5]	Therapy Traverse V5

Sand Painting and Medicine Man Boulders

Medicine Man Boulder

2. **Love Solution V3 (hb)** Climb up the center of the south face via the flake system.

3. **Good Love V4 (hb)** Start on the big bucket and climb out the top.

4. **Panic Attack V3** Climb up the center of the east face.

5. **Therapy Traverse V5** Start with the bucket and traverse to the right or start on the far-right and traverse to the left, finish with *Good Love*.

SKUNK CANYON—WEST

RASTA BOULDER
Head into the heart of Skunk Canyon, follow the narrow trail along the side of the creek, at times switching from one side to the other. This prime boulder is found in the trees, on the south side of the creek, below the second ridge of Skunk Canyon.

1. **Vibration Yeaho V6 (B2-)** Climb up the overhanging east face of the rock.

2. **Dred Arête V4** Climb the northeast arête.

BLOCK WALL
From the Rasta Boulder, cross over to the north side of the canyon and head up past the last ridge for a short ways to locate this steep block with a sheer west face.

1. **Sheer Crack V7 (hb)** Climb up the center of the west face.

2. **South Arête V4 (hb)** Climb up the arête on the southwest corner.

Rasta Boulder

Block Wall

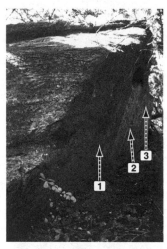

Square Rock (aka The Cube)

Hueco Boulder

HUECO ROCK

From the Rasta Boulder and Block Wall, continue up the creek line eventually curving around to the north. This boulder is located just uphill to the east and offers nice, slightly overhanging problems on its east face.

1. **Vermin Youth V4** Climb the steep wall on the far-left side of the east face.
2. **Hueco Left V5 (hb)** Climb up to the left side of the hueco then make a reach for the top.
3. **Hueco Right V5 (hb)** Climb up to the right side of the hueco then reach out to the top.

DINOSAUR MOUNTAIN

Dinosaur Mountain consists of many rock formations making up the northern slopes of Bear Canyon. There is a good selection of boulders and blocks on its eastern slopes just up and west from the Mesa Trail.

Directions: From NCAR, hike due west, eventually catching the Mesa Trail to the south. At a point before Bear Canyon's access road there is a trail heading up to the west (Mallory Cave Trail). Take this trail uphill and you find yourself staring at Square Rock. There are other boulders along the trail, past Square Rock.

SQUARE ROCK (AKA THE CUBE)

This beautiful block of maroon offers great toproping and a few highball problems. It is located just west of the Mesa Trail before reaching the Bear Canyon dirt road. Take Mallory Cave Trail (from the Mesa Trail), uphill until you run straight into it. The descent route is found on the northwest corner via a tree climb.

DINOSAUR MOUNTAIN OVERVIEW

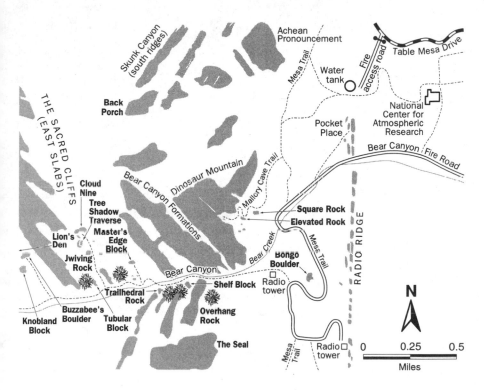

1. **Merest Excrescences V5 (hb)** Located on the west side of block. Climb up the center of the face via small crimpy holds.

ELEVATED BOULDER
Located uphill to the right (north) from the Square Rock. It sits just left of the trail.

1. **Edging Edgio V9** This starts in the overhang close to the ground on the far-left side of the rock, eventually reaching a very small crimper hold that must be utilized for a dyno to the top.

2. **Slapshot V12 (B3)** Climb the thin, overhanging, scoop-like face on the right side of the boulder.

HOLLOWAYS HANGOUT
This boulder pack is located uphill from Cube and Elevated Rock. There are many good problems on isolated boulders, as well as ridge outcrops.

Elevated Boulder   *Pocket Place*

BEAR CANYON

Bear Canyon offers some of the finest bouldering in the Flatiron Range, and lots of it. Boulders are found to the east and west of the inner canyon, as well as in the heart of it. In this book only the very best of the crop are described, starting with the Bongo Boulder to the east, the Shelf Block and Trailhedral Rock of the inner canyon, and the Master's Edge, Tubular Block, Jwiving Rock, and Cloud Nine Rock to the west. You may also access the southern spine of the Sacred Cliffs from this trail which leads up through the canyon and then out to the west, eventually intersecting the Sacred Cliffs' southern tail end.

History: All of the problems described here were put up by Bob Horan in the 1980s and 1990s.

BEAR CANYON (EAST)

These boulders and outcrops are in the meadows and hogbacks just off the Bear Canyon fire road, east of the canyon's mouth.

Directions: From NCAR, hike up to the Mesa Trail and head south until you reach the Bear Canyon Access Road. Head to the east, down the road. Looking up and to the east, you see a hogback ridge extending from north to south. The road cuts through the point where Bear Creek has formed a canyon passage through the hogback. On the north side of the ridge, you find Pocket Place. A steep trail leads from the road up to its base. On the right side of the road you see Radio Ridge.

POCKET PLACE

This overhanging outcrop is full of interesting pockets and located on the dakota sandstone hogback on the north side of the road just east of Bear Canyon.

1. **Pocket Place Traverse V5** Traverse the west face via many pockets.
2. **Finger Board Route V2** Climb the pockets on the far-right side.

Radio Ridge

The Bongo Boulder

RADIO RIDGE

This ridge offers an unlimited variety of boulder problems and traverses. It is seen extending to the south from the Bear Canyon Access Road.

1. **Radio Waves Traverse V8–V9** Traverse the underside of the west face of Radio XI Rock, located approximately 50 yards downslope from the Radio Tower.

BONGO BOULDER

From the point where the Bear Canyon Road (Mesa Trail) curves uphill to the south, continue up a short ways until the road curves back around to the north. Look down to the north in the meadow to see this big boulder sitting within the hairpin. It offers one of the Boulder area's finest traverses.

1. **Bongo Traverse V7 (B2)** From good holds down right, traverse up and across the edges.

BEAR CANYON (INNER CANYON)

The boulders and blocks of Bear's inner canyon are plentiful. A few new, quality problems have been fashioned here. Of special note are the Shelf Block and the Trailhedral Rock, located along the side of the trail.

SHELF BLOCK

On the left (south) side of the trail, as you hike into the inner canyon, the boulders and blocks begin to appear frequently. This block has an obvious overhanging shelf system on its east side.

1. **Tears Overhang V5** Climb up the center of the overhanging east face.

TRAILHEDRAL ROCK

At the far west side of the boulders and blocks along the trail, there is an overhanging spire-like rock on the left (south) side of the trail. Difficult routes ascend its north face. Descend to the southwest along the ridge.

Shelf Block

Trailhedral Rock

1. **Hydrahedral V6 (hb)** Climb right-leaning dihedral on the north face (with arête) to the top.
2. **Westside Arête V4 (hb)** Climb the northwestern arête and face of the rock.

BEAR CANYON (WEST)—INNER CANYON

These excellent boulders are found on the far-west side of Bear Canyon, past the inner canyon ridges, towards the Sacred Cliff's Southern Spine.

MASTER'S EDGE BLOCK

Follow the Bear Canyon Trail to the west, past the canyon ridges. After passing the last ridge, follow the trail west for about 50 yards until you see a couple of small boulders sitting on the right (north) side. Look up and slightly right to see a prominent bouldering block up on the northern slopes. Scramble up to its base. (See photo page 118.)

1. **Jedi Knight V7** Climb the very thin face on the left side of the south-facing wall.
2. **Master's Edge V3** Climb the arête on the far-right side of the block.

BEAR CANYON (WEST)—TREESHADOW AREA

Farther west along the Bear Canyon Trail, past a small ridge break, and a short ways upslope to the north, there is a very interesting elongated block amidst the trees. This is the first quality rock of the area, although there are others that follow up to the northeast.

Sacred Cliffs Southern Spine—Bear Canyon West Overview

(A) Hobbit Area
(B) Eden Rocks
(C) Lion's Den
(D) Sacred Cliffs Southern Spine
(E) Tree Shadow Area
    [1] Tubular Block
    [2] Jwiving Rock
    [3] Treeshadow Rock
    [4] Cloud Nine
(F) Bear Canyon West
    [1] Master's Edge Block

TUBULAR BLOCK

This steep and somewhat bulging block offers a variety of intricate face problems.

1. Easy Up V0 Climb up the far-left side of the rock, use the pedestal.

2. Slip Sliding Away V4 From thin layaways right of *Easy Up*, reach for the top.

JWIVING ROCK

This beautiful rock is found upslope from the Tubular Block, around to the east in a shallow gully. After skirting the slope up and around to the northeast, follow the

Master's Edge Block

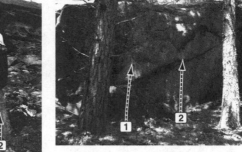

Tubular Block

western slope of the gully until you come to this, the best of the Flatiron maroons. Its south face offers amazing problems, including a traverse guaranteed to please.

1. **Jwiving to Tears V1** Climb the short face on the far-left side.

2. **Shadowed Paths V3** Climb up the center of the south face.

3. **Twaversing V5** Begin on the right side of the rock and follow the crack line down and around to the left, connecting and finishing with the *Shawdowed Paths*.

TREE SHADOW ROCK

If you continue up the fall line of big boulders from the Jwiving Rock, you almost immediately run across this large rock. Very nice traverses are found here.

1. **Treeshadow Traverse V6** Traverse the crack line from left to right.

Jwiving Rock

Tree Shadow Rock

The author sends Master's Edge *(V3), Bear Canyon West.*

Jon Anders bouldering up the Shadowed Paths (V3) on Jwiving Rock.

Cloud Nine Rock

CLOUD NINE ROCK

From Jwiving Rock and Treeshadow Rock, continue up the gully a short ways, eventually making your way into the trees. This elongated wall of rock is visible back in the trees and is reminiscent of Cloud Shadow on Flagstaff. Many vertical challenges consisting of pockets, crystals, and edges have been fashioned along its south face.

1. **Mini Bulge V3** Reach the lip and surmount the top.

2. **Number Nine Dream V2** From good finger edges behind the twisted tree, reach up to the large crystal then up to the top.

3. **Crystal's Dihedral V2** Climb the crack line within the dihedral.

4. **Crystal's Direct V2** Just right of the dihedral line, start from crystals and head straight up.

5. **Cloud Crystal V6** From two good layaway holds, reach up to a finger rapper crystal, work slightly left and up to the top.

6. **Off My Cloud V3** Climb up the overhanging face just behind the tree.

7. **Pinchildo V4** From the small finger pocket reach up to the lip and pinch it.

8. **Really V5** Reach up to the pinchy holds and flakes from the thin pockets.

9. **Little Guys V2** Utilizing the small shallow pocket make your way to the top.

FERN CANYON

Fern Canyon offers a wealth of bouldering up and through the narrows as well as great meadow bouldering to the east.

Directions: Take the Bear Canyon Road up past the Bear Canyon Trail cutoff, follow the Mesa Trail south until you reach the Fern Canyon Trail which heads up to the west. To access the Burgundy and the Megatron Boulders, head up this trail to a point before the inner canyon and head off to the south for Burgundy and the north for Megatron.

History: The problems described below were fashioned by Jim Holloway and Neil Kaptain for the Megatron and Bob Horan for the Burgundy and Fern Creek Boulders.

FERN CANYON OVERVIEW

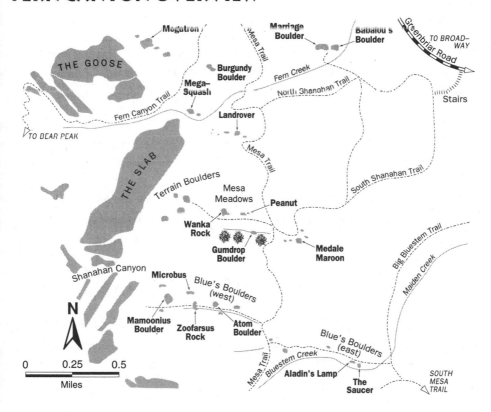

Marriage Boulder

Megatron Boulder

MEGATRON BOULDER

This boulder, sitting out below the southeastern slopes of the Goose Flatiron, is located off to the north from the trail leading up to Fern Canyon's threshold. Several other interesting large rocks will be encountered before reaching this big boulder.

1. **Kaptain's Route V3** Climb the steep, bulging face on the left side of the east face.
2. **Holloway's Overhang V6 (hb)** Climb out the large roof on the north side.

BURGUNDY BOULDER

This exceptionally nice boulder is located to the south of the Fern Canyon Trail out in the northeastern meadows of the Slab Flatiron. The demanding problems are found on its east face.

1. **Burgundy Marooner V3** Climb the face and bulge on the far-left end.
2. **Bottle of Red V4 (B1)** Climb up over the bulge right of *Burgundy Marooner*.
3. **Wine and Dine V4** Climb the thin overhang on the far-right end.
4. **Burgundy Traverse V5** Start on the far-left end and traverse to the right following a thin seam with small crimpy edges.

FERN CREEK EAST

These boulders are located on the northern slopes just off Fern Creek, east of the Mesa Trail. Take North Shanahan Trail to a point just past the halfway junction and head off to the north on a faint road descending down to the north, eventually crossing the creek.

Burgundy Boulder

MARRIAGE BOULDER

Take North Shanahan Trail a short ways past its halfway point and head across the gully to the north following a faint descending trailway/road. The two boulders are visible from the gully; they are sitting on the northern slope. The Marriage Boulder is the one on the left (west).

1. **Bachelor Pad V3** Climb the bulge on the left side of the south face.
2. **Family and the Fishing Net V4** Climb up the center.
3. **Rings of Security V2** Climb up the right side of the south face.

BABALOU'S BOULDER

This boulder sits immediately east of Marriage Boulder and is equally fun. The south-facing nature of these rocks make them a good place to boulder during winter months.

Babalou's Boulder

Land Rover Boulder

The Mega Squash

1. Necessity V2 Climb the left side of the south face via good edges.

2. Beauty Babe V3 Climb up the center of the south face via a high step.

SLAB BOULDERS

Take the North Shanahan Trail up to the Mesa Trail and head south for a short ways until reaching the first gully. Head up this gully on its northern slopes to find the Land Rover. Continue up toward The Slab to locate the Mega Squash Boulder.

History: The problems described here were fashioned by Bob Horan for the Mesa Meadows problems and Jay Droeger for The Terrain Boulders.

LAND ROVER BOULDER

This boulder is located on the north side of the Slab Gully, west of the Mesa Trail. Many boulders are located within this gully, but only a few are worthwhile. The larger of the crop are located west, up towards the main slab formation.

1. The Moon V5 Climb the south face of the boulder via very small edges.

THE MEGA SQUASH

Continue up toward The Slab to a point just before its north-end base. This big boulder is found across the gully which runs just east of The Slab's base.

1. Fall Harvest V2 (hb) Climb the northeast corner of this boulder.

2. Rise and Fall V1 (hb) Climb up the center of the east face.

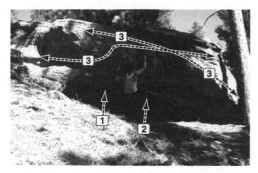

Peanut Boulder

Gumdrop Boulder

SHANAHAN CANYON

SHANAHAN NORTH—MESA MEADOWS

After taking the North Shanahan Trail up to the Mesa Trail, head south along the trail, winding around and up again until you come to a meadowesque section seen on the right (west) side of the trail. A gully lines the south side of the meadow and a small line of short boulders are on the north side. The Peanut is located up the meadow on the right, followed by Wanka Rock. The Gumdrop is across the gully on the south side of the meadow. Up beyond this, toward Slab Rock, you can see the larger block formations of the Terrain Boulders. Many good problems consisting of overhangs, traverses, as well as highball routes are to be found here.

PEANUT BOULDER

This small training rock offers many excellent challenges and is located up on the right side of the meadow.

   1. Cracker Jack V3 Climb up the overhang on left side of the south face.

   2. The Peanut V5 Climb out the center of the south face from a sit.

   3. Lusome Traverse V5 Utilizing the small crimpy edges, climb across the rock starting from low down on right and finishing up in crack at the top.

GUMDROP BOULDER

This boulder is on the south side of the gully across the meadow from the Peanut. Good north-facing problems for a hot summer's day.

   1. Bubble Gum V0 Climb up the far-left side of the north face.

Wanka Rock

2. **Jolly Rancher V1** Climb up the shielded face right of *Bubble Gum*.

3. **Starburst V3** Climb up the middle of the north face finishing up its shortened left side.

4. **Reeses Pieces V4** Climb up to the right of the center.

5. **Double Bubble V6 (hb)** Climb up the crystals right of *Reeses Pieces*.

6. **Lolly Pop V4** Climb up the far-right end of the north face.

7. **Jelly Bean V0** Climb up the west face starting at the crack.

WANKA ROCK (AKA BOB'S ROCK)

Uphill from The Peanut Boulder, the forest thins out to an open, fire-burned section of the slope. The Wanka Rock is located within this tundra-like setting. It resembles a quality Flagstaff Mountain spire, like that of Capstan Rock. A great traverse skirts its south face. Exit to the north.

1. **Golden Ticket V2 (B1-)** Climb the steep face to the left of the crack.

2. **Bob's Crack V0** This fun route climbs the crack on the south face.

3. **Wanka Traverse V5** Traverse from left to right utilizing excellent pockets and edges.

4. **Dude's Face V5 (hb)** This highball south face offers good edges.

5. **Trust Arête V5 (hb)** Climb the arête on the southeast corner.

6. **Bob's Wall V5 (hb)** Climb up the left side of the east face.

TERRAIN BOULDERS (AKA DROEGERLAND)

Continue upslope from Wanka Rock, up and slightly right heading toward the southeast corner of The Slab formation. Before reaching the Slab, you encounter several

The Ice Cube

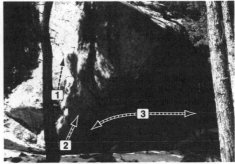

Animal Chin Boulder

blocky rocks, many of which are over thirty feet in height. Wander around and look for the chalked overhangs and traverses.

History: These boulders were developed by Jay Droeger and friends.

THE ICE CUBE (AKA FAIRVIEW BOULDER)

This is the first large block encountered while heading uphill. It is located on the north end of the slope. Look for the chalk. Problems are found on its east and north faces.

1. **Iceman Traverse V2** Traverse from the northeast corner to the far-left side.
2. **North Overhang V3** Climb out the overhang on the north side of the rock.

ANIMAL CHIN BOULDER

Continue uphill to the southwest and you run into this second large block.

1. **East Scoop V4 (hb)** Climb the steep face, left of the overhanging arête.
2. **Jay's Arête V10** Climb the overhanging arête on the northeast corner of the block.
3. **Trust Funder Traverse V0** This is a great warm-up on the north side of the block.

Note: Many more excellent problems are found within this bouldering area. Look around for the chalk.

SHANAHAN SOUTH

South Shanahan Trail: This trail takes you up to the Mesa Trail, just south of the Mesa Meadows. Just before reaching the Mesa Trail, at a point where the road takes a sharp curve heading upslope, you can see the Medale Maroon off to the south in the trees.

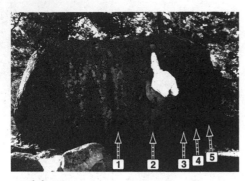

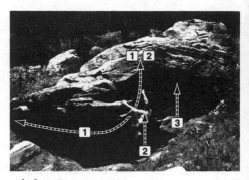

Medale Maroon   *Aladin's Lamp*

MEDALE MAROON

This beautiful piece of maroon is just east of the Mesa Trail off the South Shanahan upper trail. At a point where the South Shanahan Trail curves upslope, look to the south to see the back, north side of this gem.

1. **South Face V5** Climb up the right side of south face via small edges.
2. **Corner Stone V2** Climb the southeast corner of the block.
3. **Dice V3** Climb the east face just right of the southeast corner.
4. **East Face V2** Climb up the center of the east face.
5. **Swinger V0** On the far-right side of the east face, swing up to the top.

THE BLUES BOULDERS

This fall line of boulders offers secluded climbing sessions amidst excellent boulders. Many isolated boulders appear along this Big Bluestem trailway with a refreshing small creek nearby. Each boulder offers an amazing amount of overhanging to vertical challenges.

Directions: The lower portion of this area is accessible via the South Mesa Trailhead, located before Eldorado Canyon off Highway 170. The upper boulders are accessible via the latter or Shanahan South Trail, west of the Mesa Trail. To reach the upper section from the South Mesa Trail take Big Bluestem Trail up to Mesa Trail and then go right (north) for a short distance until you reach the next gully over. Take the gully up to the west until you run into the main boulders.

History: The problems here were put up by Bob Horan in the 1990s.

ALADIN'S LAMP

This boulder is the first challenging boulder of the far east Blues Boulders. From the South Mesa Trail, head off to the north on the Big Bluestem Trail. Take this up for a short ways until you see a few boulders just down and off the trail to the left (south).

Aladin's Lamp offers a fine array of problems in a beautifully scenic setting. In spring, the flowing creek adds to the magnificence.

1. **Genie V3** Start on the far-left side of the rock under the overhang and traverse across to the right ending at a reach problem in middle of the south face.

2. **Magic Carpet V3** Climb up the big edges in center of south face to a long reach for the top.

3. **Climb Aladin V3** Climb up the right side of the south face via small edges.

UPPER BLUES BOULDERS

These awesome boulders are located west of the Mesa Trail from the Big Bluestem Trail junction. From South Mesa Trail, take Big Bluestem Trail up west to the Mesa Trail. Head right at the Mesa Trail junction (north) for a short distance to the next gully over. Follow this up west to the boulder pack.

ATOM BOULDER

From the Mesa Trail, head up to the west. After passing a spire-like rock up the gully, head west for a short distance until you come across this super-fine chunk of maroon. Many great overhanging problems have been fashioned here.

1. **Doodlely Dud V5 (B1+)** Starting on the far-left side with the crystals in the roof, climb to the top.

2. **Curly Merl V4** Starting from the far-left, traverse up and out right.

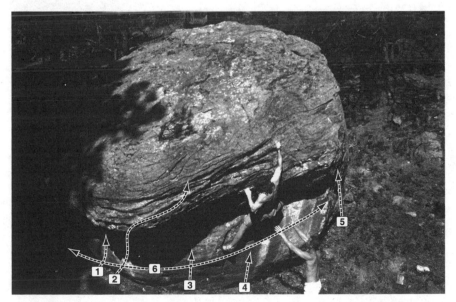

Atom Boulder

Chul Lee fires out the Zoofarsus Roof (V4), *Zoofarsus Boulder.*

Zoofarsus Boulder

3. **Mighty Dude V4** Climb the overhanging face right of *Curly Merl*.

4. **Adam's Roof V2** Climb up the center of the overhanging east face via good holds.

5. **Jumpin Gymnee V0** Climb up from the far-right side of east face.

6. **Atom Traverse V7** Traverse the length of the boulder from right to left or left to right. Back and forth for added difficulty.

ZOOFARSUS BOULDER

Continue up to the west for a short ways until you run into this unique rock. Many problems and variations have been established.

1. **Zooloo V4** Climb out the roof from the far-left side.

2. **Zoofarsus Roof V4 (B1)** Climb out the center of the boulder over the roof.

3. **Zoofarsus Traverse V6** Traverse across left to right.

4. **Zoo TV V8** Traverse from left to right finishing with *Zoofarsus Roof*.

5. **Zooper Dooper V5** Traverse across from right to left and then out *Zooloo*.

MICRO-BUS BOULDER

From the Zoofarsus Boulder, head a short ways uphill to the north until you see this chunk of natural apparatus. Many variations exist.

1. **Flower Power V4** Climb out the roof on the left side of south face.

2. **Micro Bus Traverse V4** Traverse the upper lip left to right.

MAMOONIOUS BOULDER

This large rock is located uphill approximately 100 feet, sitting within the trees. Many steep problems are found on its north and east faces. Exit on the north side.

1. **Southeast Wall V5 (hb)** Climb up the center of the southeast face.

2. **Southeast Arête V3 (hb)** Climb up to the right of *Southeast Wall*.

Micro-Bus Boulder

Mamoonious Boulder

John Baldwinn cranks the thin and steep Moonbeam *(V6), Mamoonious Boulder.*

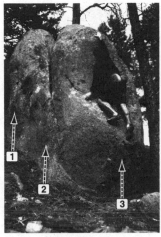

Cathedral Rock

Horan's Block

3. **Mamoonia V3 (B1)** Climb up the left side of the northeast face.

4. **Moonbeam V6** Climb the diagonaling seam right of *Mamoonia*.

CATHEDRAL ROCK
Located uphill behind and to the right of Mamoonious Boulder.

1. **Pockets V0** Climb the pockets on the left side of the west face.

2. **Bell Crack V0** Climb up the crack on the west face.

3. **Hunchback V1** Climb up the southwest slab of the rock.

MAIDEN EAST

This section of the Flatirons is best accessed from the South Mesa Trail. Take the trail due west and follow the Mesa Trail markers. After several curves in the road, you run across a bulletin board sitting very close to an old wood ruin. The Maiden is visible off to the northwest from this point. Horan's Block is located just east of the Mesa Trail from this kiosk/wood-ruin point. Head off due east into the trees. In approximately 100 feet, you encounter this block.

HORAN'S BLOCK

This quality piece of maroon offers problems comparable to those of the Milton Boulder in Eldorado Canyon. From a point along the Mesa Trail, at a kiosk and wood ruin, head off to the east from the main trail.

1. **Horse with a Name V1** Undercling the flake on the far-left end.

2. **Milestone V6 (B2-)** Climb the thin-edged face right of the undercling flake.

MAIDEN EAST AND SHADOW CANYON

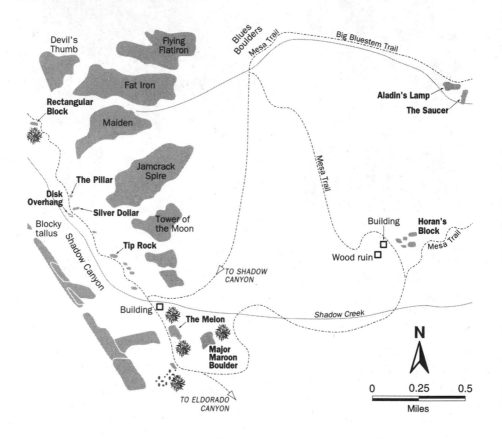

3. **At 40 V4** Climb up the thin-edged face on the right side via a high step.

4. **Swing Out V1** From the far-right end of the block step out and reach up for the top.

SHADOW CANYON

Shadow Canyon offers an enormous variety of bouldering along its steep and winding trail. I have included only a few boulders, although there are many, many more that have been bouldered upon.

Directions: Hike in from the South Mesa Trail. Follow the Mesa Trail signs west until reaching the Shadow Canyon turnoff. This trail takes you around to the backside of the Flatirons, behind the Maiden and Devil's Thumb.

History: The problems listed below were put up by Bob Horan in the early 1990s.

South Flatirons Overview

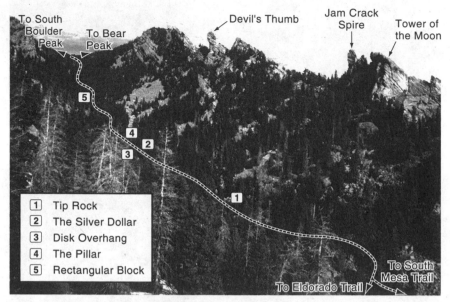

Shadow Canyon Overview

Reaching up the Coin Toss (V2) *on the Silver Dollar, Shadow Canyon.*

The Silver Dollar

Tip Rock

TIP ROCK
Found on the right side of the trail approximately 15 minutes uptrail.

    1. **South Arête V1** Climb the south arête via a small pocket and layaways.

THE SILVER DOLLAR
This oval-shaped slice of rock is found along the right side of the trail.

    1. **Silver Arête V4 (B1)** Climb the southwest arête of the rock.

    2. **Coin Toss V2** Climb up the face just right of the arête, reach for crack.

    3. **Tails It Is V1** Climb up the far-right side of the rock.

DISK OVERHANG
From the Silver Dollar, hike off to the west into the trees for a short way.

    1. **Freaky O V3** Climb out the east roof of the rock.

THE PILLAR
Found up along the trail, behind the Silver Dollar a short ways.

    1. **Southwest Arête V1** Climb the arête.

    2. **South Slab V0** Climb the south face of the block.

Disk Overhang

The Pillar

Rectangular Block

RECTANGULAR BLOCK

Continue up the trail for several hundred feet from the Silver Dollar and you come across this classic block. This is located at the top portion of the Shadow Canyon Trail. The trail cuts right in front of its north face.

1. **Rectangle V1** Climb the far-left side of the north face.
2. **Going Rectangular V1** Climb up the center of the north face.
3. **Right Rectangular V0** Climb the far-right side of the north face.

MATRON EAST

These boulders are located just off the trail (dirt road) leading up to the Shadow Canyon Trailhead junction from Eldorado or South Mesa Trailhead. The meadow setting that these boulders are found in is awesome. A great place to have a bouldering picnic.

History: The problems listed below were put in by Bob Horan in the early 1990s.

MELON BOULDER

This boulder is located just off the main trail to the east, before a hut at the beginning of the Shadow Canyon Trailhead. Difficult face climbs abound.

1. **The Edge V4** From the left side of the east face climb to the top.
2. **Underlying Dynamics V5 (B1+)** From the undercling, reach up to small edges then up to the top.
3. **Dicey Slab V4** Start right of the undercling and climb to top.
4. **Melon Arête V2** Coming in from the right reach, up to top.

Major Maroon Boulder

Melon Boulder

5. Blind Melon Corner V2 Climb the classic corner on the right side.

MAJOR MAROON BOULDER (WEST FACE)

This large boulder is located downhill, across the meadow, to the east of the Melon. The west face offers good hard face problems with perfect landings. The south face offers some fun highball routes in the V0 range. The east face offers a few exciting problems on its northeast corner. Exit the west face.

1. **Indirect West V3** Climb the far-left side of the featured west face.
2. **Direct West V4** Climb up the middle of the featured west face.
3. **Hangout V3** Climb up the right side of the west face.
4. **Easy Edge V2** Climb up the far-right side via good edges.
5. **Rollin V0** Climb to the right of *Easy Rider* via a high-step rollover.

MAJOR MAROON BOULDER (SOUTH FACE)

These are pocketed high problems on the south face.

1. **Thumbs Up V1 (hb)** Climb the pocketed face on the far-left side.
2. **Angel's Thumb V1 (hb)** Climb the left-angling crack system.

MAJOR MAROON BOULDER (NORTHEAST FACE)

There are a few problems climbing up from the face and arête of the boulder.

1. **Sheer Twist V3** Start on left side of the arête and climb up to the right.
2. **Twist To Shout V4** Climb straight up the arête, exiting on the right.

Note: A great traverse from northeast corner to west face exists.

Craig McCudden spiders his way up Thumbs Up (V1), Major Maroon Boulder.

Major Maroon Boulder, South Face

Shadow Cube

SHADOW CUBE

On the trail leading down to Eldorado Canyon from Shadow Canyon and the Mesa Trail, you come across a few gullies to the west. The Shadow Cube lies in the trees of the first gully south of the Matron. A few small boulders are visible as you come down the gully. The Shadow Cube is hidden in the trees and not visible from the main trail. You may also access this boulder by coming up from Eldorado Canyon via a trailway from out the northeast section of town.

1. **Cubular V1** Climb the cube utilizing the flake on the southeast corner.
2. **Prime Face V6** Climb up the left side of the east face.
3. **Three Leaves V4 (B1)** Climb the face and arête on the right side.
4. **Craig's Arête V1** Climb to top utilizing the far-right arête and slab.

ELDORADO CANYON

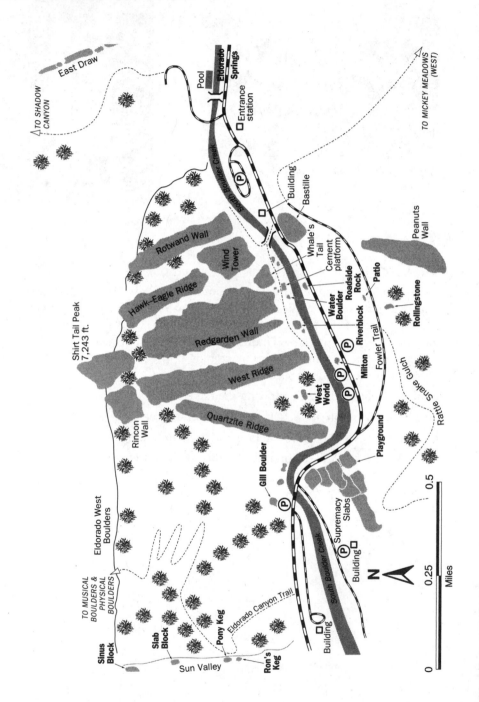

East Draw

TO SHADOW CANYON

TO MICKEY MEADOWS (WEST)

Pool

Eldorado Springs

Entrance station

Building

Bastille

Peanuts Wall

South Boulder Creek

Rotwand Wall

Wind Tower

Whale's Tail

Cement platform

Roadside Rock

Patio

Hawk–Eagle Ridge

Water Boulder

Riverblock

Rollingstone

Shirt Tail Peak 7,243 ft.

Redgarden Wall

Fowler Trail

Milton

Rattle Snake Gulch

West Ridge

West World

Quartzite Ridge

Rincon Wall

Playground

Gill Boulder

Eldorado West Boulders

Supremacy Slabs

Building

TO MUSICAL BOULDERS & PHYSICAL BOULDERS

N

South Boulder Creek

Eldorado Canyon Trail

Pony Keg

Building

Sinus Block

Slab Block

Ron's Keg

Sun Valley

0   0.25   0.5

Miles

ELDORADO CANYON

Eldorado Canyon's high quality, hardened sandstone has attracted climbers from all parts of the globe. Many rock routes with crux moves resembling boulder problems are found amidst this vertical paradise. Classic routes such as *PsychoRoof*, *Genesis*, and *Rainbow Wall*, to name a few, reflect bouldering moves executed high above the ground. These physically as well as mentally challenging routes are considered by the serious climber as mere extensions of difficult moves developed and trained for on boulders close to the ground, many of which are located within the heart of Eldorado Canyon. Eldorado's boulder problems are among the best found along the Front Range with the rock type to match. Boulder problems have been fashioned at the bases of the prominent formations as well as the many isolated boulders and blocks spread along South Boulder Creek and up its slopes. Most of these are of a hardened maroon, quality sandstone. The bouldering is extremely enjoyable for all levels of ability at any time of the year.

Directions: Go south out of Boulder on Colorado Highway 93 (Broadway). In just a few miles locate the stop light at the intersection of CO 93 and Colorado Highway 170. The Eldorado State Park sign at the intersection directs you to the west. Head west on CO 170 for approximately 3.3 miles, through the town of Eldorado Springs, until you run straight into the state park. There is an entrance station with a park official willing to collect your entrance fee. For those enjoying the canyon on a regular basis, an annual pass to the Colorado State Parks system is recommended. Otherwise, daily passes are available.

ELDORADO CANYON—INNER CANYON

THE BASTILLE

Just up the road from the entrance parking area, on the south side of the road, is the towering Bastille. In prime season you will see groups of people standing along the side of the road watching and pointing up at the entertaining boulderers and climbers. The base of the Bastille has excellent bouldering and is best known for its long traverse that skirts the base.

1. **The Shield V4 (hb)** From the east end of the Bastille's south face, walk up the road approximately 25 feet to find a smooth vertical face with small layback edges on it. Crank your way up the 20-foot face.

Bob Horan bouldering within the Eldorado Cave on Horangutan *(V5).*

The Bastille

2. **Shield Traverse V3** At the base of the Shield there is a delicate traverse with a stretchy move. This is probably the single hardest part of the lower *Bastille Traverse*.

3. **Micro Traverse V6** To the right of the *Shield Traverse* there is a delicate little edge traverse problem that skirts the ground. Stay low below the obvious rampway.

4. **March of Dimes Direct V2** Approximately 20 feet from *Micro Traverse* there is an obvious crack with a small undercling reach in it. Make the reach and proceed to the prominent left-angling finger crack (hb), or exit immediately to the right and down.

5. **Zorro Crack V3 (hb)** Just to the left of the *March of Dimes Direct* is a very thin right-angling crack that intersects the upper finger crack from *March of Dimes*.

6. **Flake Left V2** To the right of *March of Dimes Direct,* after the traverse breaks up a bit, there is a short left-leaning flake with a thin crack paralleling it on its left. Avoid the flake on the right and ascend this delicate crack.

7. **Sloper Face V2** Just right of *Flake Left,* to the right of the flake, is a small right-angling ramp system with some bolt holes at its start. Without getting too off-balance or tangled up, try to mantel your way up and across this.

8. **Lower Bastille Traverse V3 (B1)** From the far-left side of the north-facing wall, traverse across the base to the scree field on the far-right side.

The Wind Tower

THE WIND TOWER

From the entrance parking area, walk west a short ways, past the steel gate to the footbridge which leads you to the north side of the creek. The Wind Tower is visible to the northeast from the bridge. After crossing the bridge, take a right, down the trail to the east, where you find some excellent problems at the base of this large tower of rock.

1. **Wind Tower Lower Traverse V3** This mostly moderate traverse starts on the far-west side of the south face just below the *Uplift* route and traverses the entire south face.

2. **Crystal Lift V2** A polished arête with a small hollow flake at the start and a small crystal part way up. The balancey reach for the top is a real thrill.

3. **South Wall V2** There are many variations on this steep wall just right of the *Crystal Lift*. The easiest is found up a sort of groove on the left side, the middle face is classic, and the right side is a good challenge.

4. **Gold Rush V4** Across the gap from *Crystal Lift* and *South Wall* is a golden-colored, smooth vertical wall with some small edges. Crank away and mantel the top.

WHALE'S TAIL

From the north side of the footbridge, hang a left to arrive at the base of this large formation. The Whale's Tail is most famous for its large cave at the base of its west end. Some of the best bouldering is found in and around this monumental cave. The rock here is very solid and has a slick nature due to years of polishing by the river. The polished stone makes for an interesting type of bouldering, one that takes strength combined with steadiness to be successful. Of special note is the fact that all of the routes along this south face have been bouldered out by a few daring local boulderers. Although ropes are most seriously recommended for a few of these dangerously high ball (**xhb**) boulder problems, they will be included for historical reasons.

CORNERS AREA

This area encompasses the eastern portion of the Whale's Tail from *Spoof* to *Mantel Man*.

1. **Mantel Man V2–V3** As you walk west for a few feet along the eastern base of the Whale's Tail you come across a polished sloping mantel shelf. You can climb this mantel can be done in various ways. One way uses an undercling and a one-arm mantel and the other uses a straight-on, two-handed push.

2. **Slipper Face V2** Just to the left of the *Mantel Man* there is a vertical face with an undercling start leading to a down-sloping ledge system. Climb up and exit right.

3. **Dihedral 1 V2 (hb)** Just left of *Slipper Face* is a small corner with some barn door moves. You can go left or right to exit.

Whale's Tail

4. **Slick Traverse V5** Just above the ground, starting at *Dihedral 1* traverse across to *Mantel Man*.

5. **Throw Back V3 (hb)** Left of *Dihedral 1* there is an overhanging face with an arête on the left wall. Climb this and exit right.

6. **Scary Cling V3 (hb)** Just left of *Throw Back* there is a vertical wall with an interesting move at the top.

7. **Dihedral 2 V0 (hb)** Just left of *Scary Cling* there is a classic dihedral with a blocks overhang. Climb up and over, downclimb.

8. **Just Left V0 (hb)** Just to the left of *Dihedral 2* there is an overhanging face with good holds. Exit *Dihedral 2*.

9. **Pocket Bulge V1 (hb)** Left of the preceding route is a bulging wall with an obvious pocket about ten feet up.

10. **Amputee Love 5.12 V6 (xhb)** A toprope problem that was bouldered out by Darius Azin in 1990. Start to the left of pocket bulge, right of *Spoof* ramp, and climb the steep, overhanging face via slopey edges.

CREEK SLAB

Across the trail from the *Mantel Man* problem on the Whale's Tail, there is a big boulder with a smooth northeast-facing slab. Many problems exist on this slab, as well as many little edges. Most problems are in the V0 to V1 range.

CREEK BOULDER

Just west of the Creek Slab, there is a nice rounded boulder with a difficult east-facing bulge. In high-water season the start is submerged.

Creek Slab

Creek Boulder

1. **East Bulge V5 (B1+)** From the sandy beach below the retaining wall you will notice an east-facing bulge with some delicate layback edges. Climb up and mantel.

THE CAVE AREA

These boulder problems are found in and around the cave's threshold. Continue west along the base of the Whale's Tail and you can't miss this cave.

1. **Cave Traverse V7** From the back of the cave traverse out toward the opening via laybacks, underclings, knee locks, and iron cross moves.

2. **Threshold Traverse V4** Traverse the outer threshold of the cave close to the ground.

3. **The Monument 5.12 V5 (xhb)** A lead route bouldered out by Gary Ryan in the early '90s. Undercling up and out, finishing at the top of *Horangutan*.

4. **Horangutan 5.12 V5 (xhb)** Another lead route bouldered out by Bob Horan in 1984, begin at the mouth of the cave on the big holds and climb up and out diagonally left.

5. **Around the World V3 (B1)** On the east side of the cave, at its opening, there is a polished wall. This is the rightmost section of the *Cave Traverse*. Traverse in a circular direction utilizing the good but angling edge system.

6. **Ironman V6** Left of *Around the World*, this climbs up small holds with an iron cross reach out right of the bulge to the big jugs of *Around the World*.

Whale's Tail west end, left to right: N.E.D. Wall, Cave Area, Corners Area.

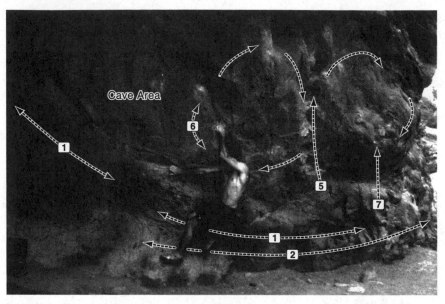

Cave Area

7. **Vertical Polish V3** In the middle of the *Around the World* problem there is a face with some small edges that can be ascended by utilizing a tricky mantel.

N.E.D. WALL
Outside the cave to the west is a beautiful wall with a wide variety of problems.

1. **N.E.D. 5.12 V5 (xhb)** Another lead route bouldered out by Bob Horan in 1984. Climbs out the severe overhang via dynamic moves up and left of the cave's threshold.

2. **Off the Couch V1** Below and slightly left of the *N.E.D.* roof there is a slightly overhanging face with some nice little jugs on it. Exit right, or left to *Clementine*.

3. **Clementine V0 (hb)** Just left of *Off the Couch* is an obvious crack line that fades left onto some polished ledges.

4. **Lunge Break V2 (B1-)** Just left of *Clementine* directly across from the northeast corner of the cement platform, there is a bulging, sloping ledge system. There are many different eliminates to gain the sloping ledges, including a double lunge.

5. **Double Lunge V6** From two good holds, left of the start of *Lunge Break*, soar up with two hands, latch onto the sloping edges, and finish *Lunge Break*.

6. **Smooth One V8** This problem climbs up from the left of *Double Lunge* utilizing very small edges in the bulge.

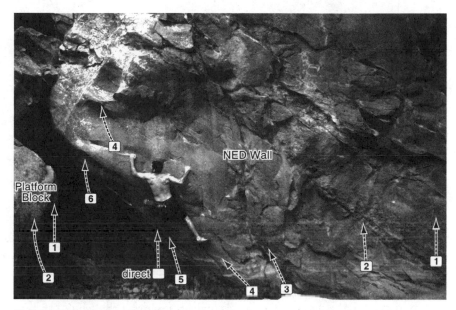

N.E.D. Wall, Platform Block

PLATFORM BLOCK

This block is immediately west of the far southwest corner of the Whale's Tail, forming somewhat of a cave between the two.

1. **The Arête V2** Just left and slightly south, almost touching the *Lunge Break* problem there is a short arête with a tricky heel hook move.

2. **Micro Pull V7** To the immediate left of *The Arête* there is a short bulging wall. Feel up for the micro edges if you can reach them and pull to the top.

3. **The Layback V0** From a sitting position left of *Micro Pull* there is a short layback problem.

CLOSE TO THE EDGE BLOCKS

Immediately up and left of N.E.D. Wall, above the Platform Block, there are two elongated blocks. The lower block offers several difficult mantels as well as a traverse that is linked with the upper block. The upper block has an upward diagonaling arête.

1. **Mondoman Traverse V6** From the far-west edge of the lower rock, traverse across and then link upward with the *Close to the Edge* problem.

Close to the Edge Blocks

2. Close to the Edge V4 (B1) This upper diagonal, right-leaning arête's edge traverse makes its way up the upper block.

WATER BOULDER

From the cement platform at the southwest corner of the Whale's Tail, the trail continues west along the creek. After about 50 feet, near a small cement dam you discover this nice block with a sheer northwest face. Many problems exist all around this, including an exciting traverse over the water.

1. **East Arête V2** On the easternmost edge of the boulder there is a right-leaning face.

2. **Center Route V3** This is a tricky layaway problem up the center.

3. **West Side V2** Just right of the *Center Route* there is another small-edged challenge.

4. **Undercling Face V1** On the far-right side of the boulder there is a fun undercling route that consists of a high step and long reach.

5. **Water Boulder Traverse V4** This is a traverse of the lower northwest face of the boulder. Little edges and footholds make this a great challenge. On the west side of the rock there is a fun low-angle slab with some good friction. This is also the easiest descent from the top.

6. **Over Water Traverse V1** On the south face of the boulder, over the water, there is a nice set of holds that can be traversed and ascended via a small layback system. Start west and head east and up.

BARREL BLOCK

Just to the east of the Water Boulder there is a barrel-shaped polished block with some thin problems on its west face. The rock that has fallen against its north end also has some challenging roof moves.

MONKEY BOULDER

This boulder is located on the hillside north of the Barrel Block. The west overhang has an incredible swinging move (V3) to gain its summit.

ROADSIDE OVERHANG

From the Water Boulder, across Eldorado Creek to the southwest, there is a hidden overhang sitting just below the roadway.

1. **Standard V2** This is the easiest way out of the overhang and finishes over the lip utilizing good pockets. Start in the center of the roof.

2. **Psychit Roof V4** This is a direct roof problem with counter pulls to gain the lip. Start left of *Standard*.

A Water Boulder
2 Center Route (V3)
6 Over the Water Traverse (V0)
B Monkey Boulder
C Barrel Rock
D Close to the Edge Blocks
E Platform Block
F NED Wall

Boulders West of Whale's Tail

Roadside Overhang

Crank Rock

CRANK ROCK

This overhanging block is located upcreek from the Water Boulder on the same (north) side. Follow the trail slightly uphill and then cut across a faint path leading down along the creek. This south-facing wall emerges from out the creek bed. In spring and midsummer the base will most likely be under water.

1. **Crankakee V3 (hb)** On the south face of the rock, climb the overhanging face via sloping holds. Other variations exist.

RIVER BLOCK

Getting back to the main trail, on the north side of the creek, follow it west past the lower south end of the Red Garden Wall for about 200 feet. From here drop down toward the creek to this massive block which sits along the creekbed. Look for challenging problems on its south and east faces.

River Block

Cranking off the radically difficult Kiss of Life (V7) *on the River Block.*

1. **Gunk Roof V1** On the upper slope of the east side of the block, hidden in the bush somewhat, there is an incredible set of good holds leading out right to the dicey lip. The ground is close enough for comfort.

2. **Kiss of Life V7 (hb)** On the lower east side of the block is a large roof with a little jam in it. From here, you must reach up to the sloping ledge and mantel to a stance. The rest is airy but moderate.

3. **Eastern Priest V4 (hb)** On the south face of the boulder, just out of the creek, there is an overhanging face with some scary reaches.

4. **Fall Line V0** Left of *Eastern Priest* there is a classic crack. Laybacking this line is a true delight.

MILTON BOULDER

This is one of Eldorado's true prizes and is located about 200 yards up the road from the Bastille. The boulder sits along the north side of the road with a blank looking southwest face. Many incredible routes are all around this gem. Some of Eldorado's most difficult face problems have been fashioned here.

1. **Ridge Face V0** On the far-left side of the west face there is a thin slab with some delicate moves.

2. **Layaway V0** This is probably the easiest way to ascend the west face. Start out on a big step just off the ground and follow the laybacks up and right, around the overhang at the top.

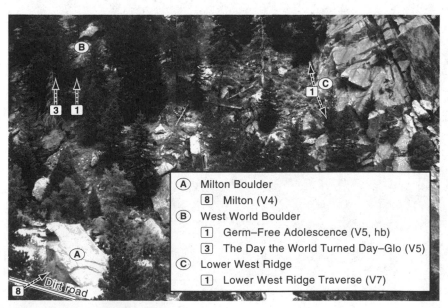

Milton Boulder and West World Boulder

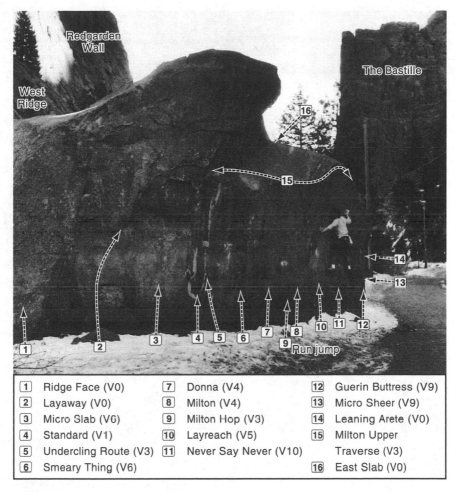

Milton Boulder

1	Ridge Face (V0)	7	Donna (V4)	12	Guerin Buttress (V9)
2	Layaway (V0)	8	Milton (V4)	13	Micro Sheer (V9)
3	Micro Slab (V6)	9	Milton Hop (V3)	14	Leaning Arete (V0)
4	Standard (V1)	10	Layreach (V5)	15	Milton Upper
5	Undercling Route (V3)	11	Never Say Never (V10)		Traverse (V3)
6	Smeary Thing (V6)			16	East Slab (V0)

3. Micro Slab V6 To the right of *Layaway* there is a thin slab with no footholds and very small edges. Climb up and exit right.

4. Standard V1 To the right of *Micro Slab* there is a thin face following a crack.

5. Undercling Route V3 To the right of the *Standard* route there is a conspicuous undercling which can be used to gain the upper slopes of the boulder.

6. Smeary Thing V7 Immediately right of the *Undercling Route* there is a strenuous friction problem that ascends the scoop. Start by pinching the arête, throw a smeary stem out right, reach a small layaway just inches right of the undercling, reach for the slopey shelf above a mantel.

Mark O'Brien twinkling his toes up the Milton *(V4), Eldorado Canyon.*

7. **Donna V4** This was named for the graffiti once below its face. To the right of the Smear Thing route there is another thin finger problem that uses a two-finger, left-handed nitch. High step and reach for the top, then mantel.

8. **Milton V4 (B1)** This is the center problem on the southwest face and was named after the writing once on the southwest wall, hence the boulder's name, as well. Pull on the face with a good layback and reach up for an obvious crystal and edge, go for the top and mantel.

9. **Milton Hop V3** This is a run and jump problem, up the *Milton* face that latches the mantel shelf.

10. **Layreach V5** Immediately right of the *Milton* there is a good right-hand layback hold. Smear up to this and crank to the top.

11. **Never Say Never V10 (B2+)** This is the blank-looking scooping face to the right of the *Milton* problem. This problem had been unsuccessfully tried for years, until Jim Ratzlaph ran up and slam dunked the top. Although this was rather exciting to watch, the problem done this way, was height and jump strength dependant. Later Steve Mammen worked the top face off cheat stones and was able to climb all but the start move. Eventually he figured out a dynamic jump start which awkwardly set him upon the wall. Bob Horan originally worked it with him this way but still thought the problem should go more smoothly at the start. Shortly thereafter, Horan sent it from a static start off the ground, utilizing a downpressing mantel move with his right hand while latching the layaway with his left.

12. **Guerin Buttress V9** This thin problem laybacks the prow right of the *Never Say Never*.

13. **Micro Sheer V9** On the south face of the boulder there is an improbable-looking face that crimps small holds to the top.

14. **Leaning Arête V0** On the south side of the boulder, just right of *Micro Sheer*, there is a left-leaning arête. Keep your body on the left side and traverse up to the top.

15. **Milton Upper Traverse V3** On the top edge of the southwest face you can traverse back and forth until totally pumped.

EAST SLAB

On the east side of the Milton Boulder there is an excellent beginner's slab with many variations, including "no hands" for a good challenge.

WEST WORLD

Across from the Milton Boulder to the north, upslope in the trees, is a cluster of boulders. During high water you must access this area by crossing the footbridge toward the Whale's Tail, heading to the west down the main trail, and continuing

Lower West Ridge

The Playground

past the West Ridge. In low-water season you can access the area by crossing the creek at the Milton Boulder.

LOWER WEST RIDGE

On the lower southern end of the West Ridge there is an awesome traverse skirting the base. Hike uphill on the main trail past the West Ridge. The traverse is found along the trail about 100 feet up from the creek.

1. **West Ridge Traverse V6** Follows the crack line from right to left.
2. **Terminator Version V7** Starts on the crystalline wall right of the crack line adding several meters of hard crystal crimping in the bulging wall, finish with *West Ridge Traverse.*

WEST WORLD BOULDER

Hike west from Lower West Ridge Traverse, off the main trail toward the trees, to discover this obvious roof-like overhang with a good flake system leading out its lip.

1. **Germ-Free Adolescence V5 (B1+) (hb)** Climb the extreme south-facing roof with a tree close by. Yard on the flake system to the edges in the roof. The scary part is turning the lip.
2. **Here Comes Sickness V8 (hb)** This problem climbs the *Germ-Free Adolescence* problem overhang (from a sitting position) connecting to the top.
3. **The Day the World Turned Day-Glo V5** Just to the left of *Germ-Free Adolescence* there is a bulging wall with a delicate move to gain the top.
4. **Genetic Engineering V5** This is another bulge problem just to the left of the *Day Glo* bulge.

West World Boulder

THE HIGH SPIRE (NOT PICTURED)

Just behind and to the northeast of West World Boulder is this twenty-five-foot spire. An obvious crack system starts on its southwest corner and then angles up to the right.

1. **High Spire Crack V2 (hb)** This very committing problem takes the obvious crack system on the south face of the spire.

THE PLAYGROUND

Up the road from the Milton Boulder, to the point where the road levels off and turns to the north, a roadcut is encountered. On the roadcut's south side, a short ways upslope to the west and facing southwest, there is a quartzite wall with good problems including a 140-foot traverse.

1. **Natural Pro Traverse V3** Starting at the lower right end of the formation, traverse low for 140 feet up the slope. For an extra pump traverse back down the slope. Other more difficult eliminations exist.

FOWLER TRAIL BOULDERS

From the small parking lot for the Playground, head up to the south and then east along the Fowler Trail, past the Rattlesnake Gulch junction for about 100 feet. These boulders are located up on the right and down to the left, somewhat close to the trail.

Rolling Stone Rock

ROLLING STONE ROCK

From the Milton Boulder, head uproad to the west and catch the Fowler Trail heading back east past the Rattlesnake Trail junction for approximately 100 feet. This unique boulder is visible from the trail when looking up on the southern slope. The boulder's postion allows for difficult traversing up its leaning eastern arête.

1. **High Traverse V6** Start on the far-right and traverse the boulder staying up and along the lip.

2. **Sticky Fingers V7** Start as for *High Traverse* problem but drop down into the roof holds and then across low.

3. **Rolling Roof V4** From a sitting position climb up and out to the top, then across to the left for finish.

4. **Stoned Roof V3** Climb the roof via large holds in the ceiling, finish by traversing left.

PATIO BOULDER (NOT PICTURED)

This boulder is located just downtrail to the east, on the north side, below an old stone wall. Good problems exist in this semi-secluded place. The problems are somewhat highball. A spotter and pad are recommended.

1. **Patio Arête V3 (hb)** Climb the left arête of the north face.

2. **The Patio V3 (hb)** Climb up center of north face via good edges.

3. **Patio Right V2** Climb right side of north face.

Water Rock

Supremacy Rock

SUPREMACY ROCK

From the Milton Boulder continue up the road past the Playground and roadcut, then down to the intersection at the bridge over Eldorado Creek. Supremacy Rock is along the side of the road, on the left, where the road takes a turn to the left before the bridge. A fun traverse along its base offers good warm-up and eliminates.

WATER ROCK

From the bridge near Supremacy Rock, look to the southwest to see this rock sitting on the east side of the creek with its oval-shaped west face.

1. **West Scoop V0 (hb)** This is the obvious west face with a crystal jug halfway up the face. Many other variations are possible.

THE GILL BOULDER

This challenging, very diverse boulder is hidden in the trees just northeast of the bridge. All sides of this classic blocky boulder have great problems with good landings. Descend on the west side via a tree step.

WEST FACE GILL BOULDER

1. **Western Slab V0** On the southwest corner of the boulder there is a narrow slab leading to the top.
2. **Ament's Wall V4** Right of the prominent descent tree is a vertical wall with a hard move off some small edges eventually reaching the top.

The Gill Boulder

NORTH FACE GILL BOULDER

3. Gill Face V4 (B1) Around to the left of the *Ament's Wall* there is a smooth vertical wall immediately left of the northwest corner.

4. Baldwin Face V5 Left of the *Gill Face* about 10 feet there is a thin-edged face. Move up and right.

5. Standard Route V3–V4 This is the obvious vertical face up the center of the sheer north face.

6. Horan Face V6 Just left of the *Standard Route* there is a set of small edges. Climb up and slightly right finishing at the top of the *Standard Route*.

7. Northeast Reach V0 On the northeast corner of the boulder there is an exciting route that starts out with some great edges with a long reach to the top.

EAST FACE GILL BOULDER

1. East Dihedral V0 On the east side of the boulder there is an obvious dihedral leading up to the top.

The Gill Boulder, West and South Face

2. Southeast Corner V0 This short but fun route climbs the southeast corner via some laybacks.

3. East Side Traverse V0 This is a good traverse that skirts the east face of the boulder, the most difficult section being at the north end.

SOUTH FACE GILL BOULDER

1. South Left V3 On the left side of the slab there's a thin face that is gained with a small toe pocket and high step.

2. South Center V4 This is a very difficult thin-edged face up the center of the slab.

3. South Right V3 On the far-right side of the thin slab there's a delicate face requiring a thumbs-down push and small step.

ELDORADO WEST

To reach Eldorado West, continue up the road to the north from the Gill Boulder (located in the back of Eldorado Canyon), and take the Eldorado Canyon Trail up toward Rincon Wall. Along this trail, which eventually extends below Cadillac Crag, The Veil, and Physical Crag, you will encounter several bouldering areas. The first area at the lower portion of the trail is the Sun Valley. Next, after hiking up trail farther and eventually passing the Rincon Wall access cut-off, you will encounter the Musical Boulders, which are found downslope to the west of the trail. Continuing

ELDORADO WEST

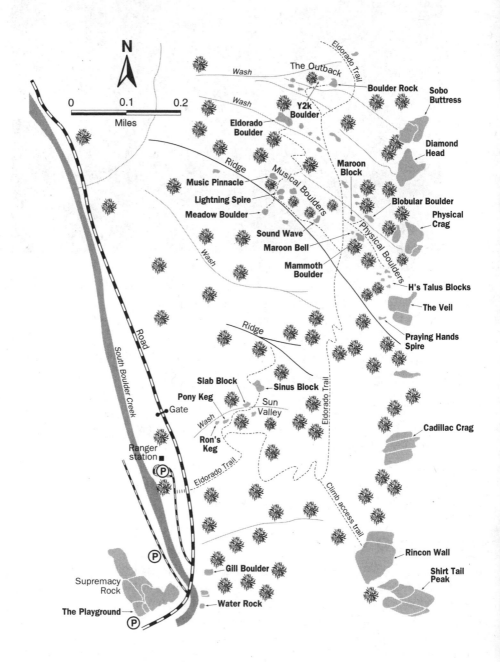

N

0   0.1   0.2

Miles

The Outback

Eldorado Trail

Wash

Boulder Rock

Sobo
Buttress

Wash

Y2k
Boulder

Eldorado
Boulder

Diamond
Head

Ridge

Musical Boulders

Maroon
Block

Music Pinnacle

Lightning Spire

Blobular Boulder

Meadow Boulder

Physical
Crag

Physical Boulders

Sound Wave

Maroon Bell

Mammoth
Boulder

H's Talus Blocks

Wash

The Veil

Ridge

Praying Hands
Spire

Road

Slab Block

Sinus Block

Pony Keg

Sun
Valley

Eldorado Trail

South Boulder Creek

Gate

Cadillac Crag

Wash

Ron's
Keg

Ranger
station

(P)

Eldorado Trail

Climb access trail

(P)

Rincon Wall

Gill Boulder

Shirt Tail
Peak

Supremacy
Rock

Water Rock

The Playground

(P)

The author bouldering on one of the many blocks on the slopes of Eldorado West.

along the trail to the north you will find the Physical Boulders (aka Horan's Hangout) and then the Outback Boulders located even farther north.

SUN VALLEY

Hike up the Eldorado Canyon Trail for approximately one tenth of a mile until you come to a point where you can easily access the first gully on the left (north) side of the trail. Hike thirty feet down to the wash and you will see the first of the Sun Valley Boulders in the meadow. Follow this fall line of boulders east.

RON'S KEG BOULDER

This is the first of the lot and has great huecos on its sides. Several lines exist, including a traverse.

PONY KEG BOULDER

This is located just east of Ron's Keg Boulder and offers excellent challenges.

1. **Pony Keg Traverse V8-9** Traverse the rock from left to right.
2. **Days of Past, Present V4** Climb out the center of the overhanging north face.
3. **Woody's Crystal V3** Climb the steep slab up the middle of the west face.

(A) The Egg
(B) The Pinnacle
(C) Lightning Spire
(D) Sound Wave Boulder

Musical Boulders

SLAB BLOCK

This block has a steep and thin southwest-facing slab and is located about 100 feet up the gully from the Pony Keg Boulder.

1. Freaky Slab V5 A reach problem that turns onto the thin slab above.

SINUS BOULDER

Continue up the gully from the Slab Block for about 150 feet and you will encounter this nice, bulging boulder with a classic traverse crack splitting its southwest face.

MUSICAL BOULDERS

These nice boulders offer a wide variety of problems consisting of face and pocket challenges. To locate the Musical Boulders, continue up the Eldorado Canyon Trail past the Rincon Wall's trail junction. Travel down trail for a while and then up again. The boulders are downslope to the west from where the trail peaks out at a prominent grassy ridge. Descend down to the boulders at that point.

SOUND WAVE BOULDER

This is the first of the boulders reached when heading downslope from the main trail.

1. Sound Wave Traverse V5 Traverse the base of this boulder via side pulls and pinch grips.

Sound Wave Boulder

Lightning Spire

LIGHTNING SPIRE (AKA HERTZ ROCK)

Continue a short ways downhill into the trees and you run straight into this spire.

1. **Midnight Frightening Arête (Project)** Climb up the severely overhanging arête on the far-right side of the north face.

THE MUSIC PINNACLE

A short distance downhill from Lightning Spire, look for this nice pinnacle with good problems on its south and north faces.

1. **Pinnacle Crack V0** Climb the crack and pockets on the south face. *Note:* Also the descent route.

2. **East Seam V2** Climb the obvious seam to top of the pinnacle.

3. **East Face Center V2–V3** Climb the north face, right of the seam, via crystals and edges.

4. **East Face Arête V3** Climb the arête on right side of the north face to the top.

MEADOW BOULDER (AKA THE EGG)

This is perhaps the best boulder of the crop with excellent routes found all around the egg shaped spired boulder. From the Pinnacle, head due south for about 100 yards to run into this awesome boulder.

WEST FACE

1. **West Center V2** Climb up the west face to the top.

2. **West Right V1** Climb up the right side of the west face.

The Music Pinnacle

Meadow Boulder (The Egg), west face

EAST FACE

3. **Southeast Buttress V5 (hb)** Climb the steep face on the far-left side.

4. **East Face V3** Climb up the right side of the east face.

THE ELDORADO BOULDER

From the Music Boulders Area you must head downslope to the north. Traverse the slope down to a point that will eventually lead you deep into the gully. This boulder is perhaps the largest in the area and offers excellent highball problems, as well as close-to-the-base problems.

1. **The Streaked Corner V4 (hb)** Climb the obvious corner problem on the west face.

2. **Fantastic Face V0** Climb the edges to the right of *The Streaked Corner*, exit to the right.

PHYSICAL BOULDERS (AKA HORAN'S HANGOUT)

Continue along the Eldorado Trail, past the point where you would descend down to the Musical Boulders. The trail will lead you downslope a short distance eventually leveling out in a thick forested area packed with boulders. This is the halfway point of the huge fall line of boulders that begins at the base of the Veil and Physical Crag's Formations and extends downslope to the west, all the way to South Boulder Creek and the canyon floor. From this point travel upslope into the trees for some real nice bouldering surprises.

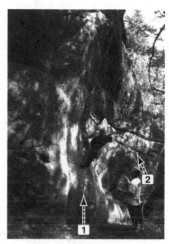

Meadow Boulder (The Egg),
east face

The Eldorado Boulder

THE MAROON BLOCK

From the trail within the forested boulder pack, head upslope to the east into the trees. After approximately 150 feet you will see this awesome, 20-foot overhanging, maroon-colored block. This is one of the nicest piece of maroon Eldorado has to offer. Starting from left to right there is a quality line every four feet adding up to twelve individual problems to date. Problems range from V1 to V8.

BLOBULAR BOULDER

From the Maroon Block continue upslope to the northeast for approximately 100 yards and you will find the large, rounded boulder with a sheer south face and an overhanging west side. Problems have been done all around this rock and are well worth the visit.

NOTE: Continuing up and down this fall line from Physical Boulder, The Maroon Block or Blobular Boulder you will encounter an endless array of good quality boulders and blocks with a wide range of challenges.

MAROON BELL

To the right of the Maroon Block (approximately 100 feet south) you will find a smaller maroon-colored block with more moderate crack and face routes up its west face.

MAMMOTH BOULDER

Behind the Maroon Bell a short distance you will find a huge boulder with a traverse located close to the ground.

THE OUTBACK

From the point along the Eldorado Trail where you cross the Physical Boulders fall line, continue along the trail to the north to a location where the trail takes a sharp turn to the east. At this point travel downslope to the northwest, into the trees and toward the gully below; soon you will encounter other fine rocks with good landings.

THE Y2K BOULDER

Once in the gully head upslope to the east until you reach the top of a hidden ridge. This boulder is located within the trees and offers great crystal and edge climbing all around.

BOULDER ROCK

From the Y2K Boulder head farther east for approximately 50 feet and you will see this awesome rock hidden in the trees. Great traversing and bulge climbing are offered all around its base.

CLOUD NINE

This area, packed with many Flagstaff-type outcrops and a fair selection of isolated boulders, is actually located due west of the Mickey Mouse Wall Summit, and northwest of the Radio Tower. The hike is involved and takes approximately one hour and forty-five minutes. To approach the area, you must access it via Eldorado Canyon State Park beginning at the Fowler Trail Trailhead.

History: Much of the development was done by Mike Brooks, Chip Ruckgaber, John Baldwinn, Matt Samet, and Eric Johnson, to name a few, as well as others.

Directions: Drive into Eldorado State Park, up past the Bastille to the Playground bouldering wall. Park there and head up the Fowler Trail, then take the Rattlesnake Gulch Trail up to the west. Follow the trail up to the hotel ruin at approximately 1.2 miles, then up to the divide lookout. Approximately 100 yards before the lookout, take the turnoff left (south) onto Rattlesnake Gulch Loop Trail. Walk south for a few minutes, then follow a cutoff to the west onto the ridge. Walk along the ridge for approximately 100 feet and take the trail horizontally (south) toward the train tracks. Take this faint trail for a good ten minutes until you drop down into a gulch. Cut right at a marker and go over the creek wash. Head to the west for approximately 20 feet then turn left onto the steep hillside. An old trail goes up this hillside. Begin to switchback up until you reach the knoll. Continue south up switchbacks to a grassy saddle, then head southwest toward the tracks. Drop down a scree slope above tunnel number 12's entrance. Cross the tracks and walk along the left side until you see another faint trail cutting back southeast into the valley, just before the entrance to tunnel 13. Hike along for approximately 50 yards, then drop into the middle of the gulch. Look for the pink ribbons leading you to the south and up. Follow the steep

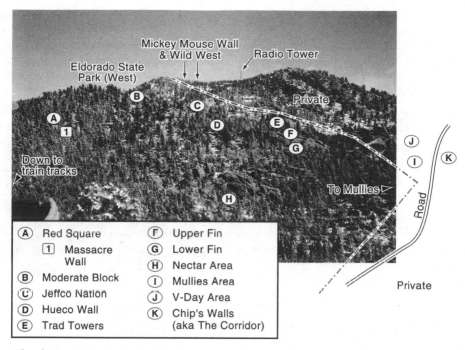

Cloud Nine Overview, aka C4 Area

trail up the valley for approximately ten minutes, then cut right onto an eroding quartzite hillside and bust straight up for the ridge for approximately five to ten minutes. Continue to follow the pink ribbons along the ridge, through the thick forest, for approximately ten minutes until you reach a high shoulder that is home to the Bear Track Boulder.

Note: If these directions seem confusing, it would be a good idea to go with someone who knows how to get there. Directions were given by the developers of the area. Most of the good rock is down the hill to the south from the high point of the approach hike. Take the high trail to reach the Hueco Wall and other upper areas. Take the low trail to reach the Nectar Area, the Lower and Upper Fins, Entry Rock, and Knobular Wall.

MULLIES AREA

This is the southernmost area of Cloud Nine, very close to the dirt road at the crest of the ridge. At the ridge crest, where the road is, head off into the trees for approximately 50 yards to locate this long bouldering wall. Landings are very good.

Mullies Area

MULLIES WALL

This light brown, north-facing wall stretches approximately 150 feet and is filled with problems. The left (east) side is more flake- and edge-like, while the right (west) side is very crystalled.

1. **Mullies Right V0** Climb the crease on the left side of the north face.

2. **Sharp Flakes V1** Climb the obvious flake system in the middle of the wall.

3. **Super Classic V2** Climb the jutting crystals on the right side.

THE CORRIDOR

Across the road to the west from Mullies is a group of finned ridges. Many traverses and crystal routes are evident.

V-DAY BLOCK (NOT PICTURED)

Slightly downslope, east of Mullies Wall, you find this prize maroon block.

1. **Pockets Left V5** Climb up the left side utilizing pockets, then work right past a mono-divot.

2. **Hueco Classic V0** Climb up the huecos in the middle of the east face.

3. **Black Seam V4–V5** Climb the faint seam in the black streak.

The Corridor

Hueco Wall Area

HUECO WALL AREA

Approximately 150 feet to the east of Mullies Wall, up the gully slots, Look for this awesome huecoed traverse wall. This is the favorite warm-up wall at Cloud Nine.

1. **Hueco Wall Traverse V1–V2** Traverse the wall right to left via large bucket holds.

WOOTANG'S BOULDER GARDEN

From Mullies Wall, head down to the northeast through the forest and you run into this boulder field. A few good problems have been done here.

WOOTANG'S ROCK

This fine cone-shaped block has a great north face with good face problems.

1. **Wootang Ridge V0** Climb the right-angling edge system up the left side of the north face.

2. **I like Woo V3** Climb the steep face on the far-right side.

Wootang's Rock

Notch Boulder   *Massacre Wall*

THE SANCTUARY

Uphill from the Hueco Wall, to the northeast approximately 50 yards, work your way through the ridgebreak to this hidden coved area.

NOTCH BOULDER

Within the Sanctuary there is a large brown, 25-foot block with black streaks in it. The landing zone is soft and flat.

1. **Deathco Nation V6** Climb the micro sidepulls in the black streak on the left side, finish to the right.
2. **Jeffco Nation V3** Climb up the jugs in the middle of the face, reach for a pebble, then left on crimps and up to the huecoed top.

LOWER FIN (NOT PICTURED)

This fin is in the trees below the Hueco Wall, to the northwest.

1. **Purple People Eater V8** Crank the powerful face via small tweakers on the purple shield of the fin's north end.
2. **Fingus V3** Climb to the right along the horizontal then up the finger seam.

UPPER FIN

Another problematic fin with enough problems to please all levels of ability.

Big Boy Block

White Crystal Dome

MASSACRE WALL

From the Fins, head across to the east and slightly down to the north until you run across these outcroppings and boulders hidden in the trees. The main events are located at the tail end, northwest side of the elongated outcrop.

1. **Massacre V3** Climb up the direct crack line in the middle of the scooped shield at the tail end of the outcrop.

2. **Indirect V2** Climb the better edges to the right of *Massacre*.

BIG BOY BLOCK

Continue up the ridge to the north end to find this classic cube of maroon. A larger formation rises behind it.

1. **Big Boy Arête V2** Climb the arête on the far-left side of the west face.

2. **Jealous Companions V0** Climb up the center of the west face.

3. **Loser Friends V0** Climb up the face on the right side.

WHITE CRYSTAL DOME

Below and slightly west of the Big Boy Block there is a sheer, dome-shaped block with a few white crystals on its north face.

1. **Lilly White Lilith V6** Climb up the center of the north face utilizing the crystals.

Note: This area has many, many more rocks and problems and is still in its early development. The hillside here would easily make this place a rival hotspot. Good thing the hike is too long for most people. Keep the place clean and don't disturb the surroundings.

MICKEY MOUSE MEADOW OVERVIEW

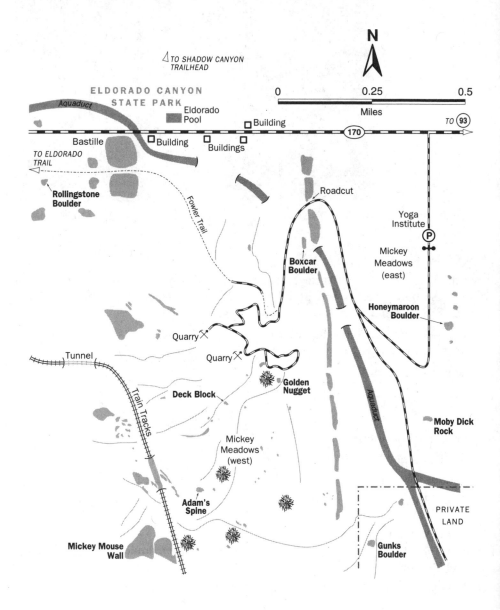

△ TO SHADOW CANYON
TRAILHEAD

N

ELDORADO CANYON
STATE PARK

Aquaduct

Eldorado
Pool

0   0.25   0.5
Miles

TO 93

Building

Bastille

Building

Buildings

170

TO ELDORADO
TRAIL

Rollingstone
Boulder

Fowler Trail

Roadcut

Yoga
Institute

P

Boxcar
Boulder

Mickey
Meadows
(east)

Honeymaroon
Boulder

Quarry

Tunnel

Quarry

Train Tracks

Deck Block

Golden
Nugget

Aquaduct

Moby Dick
Rock

Mickey
Meadows
(west)

Adam's
Spine

PRIVATE
LAND

Mickey Mouse
Wall

Gunks
Boulder

MICKEY MEADOWS

MICKEY MOUSE MEADOW (EAST)

This meadow offers isolated boulders with good landings. The best time of year to boulder on these rocks is late fall and throughout the winter months. Other times of year, the grass is too high and there are too many mosquitos.

Directions: Just before entering the town of Eldorado Springs, off CO 170 (see directions to Eldorado Canyon), there is a road leading off to the south (left) from the main road. It is marked with a small sign that reads "Yoga" at its beginning. Turn up this road and take it to the end. There is a small parking area at the trailhead for this now-official Open Space area. The boulders ahead lie on the left side of the dirt-road trail. The first boulder, the Honey Maroon Boulder, is about 200 yards ahead on the east side of the small creek. Moby Dick Rock is best accessed by hiking farther up the road around several curves until it heads back to the south.

HONEY MAROON BOULDER

This is the first of the worthwhile boulders up the road on the left (east) side of the creek. Many good problems are found, including a classic overhanging crack on its northwest corner.

1. **The Scoop V4** Climb the scooping north face of the boulder to crystals above.

2. **Pebbled Shield V4** Start in the crack and reach out left to crystals.

3. **Earth Crack V2 (B1-)** Climb the classic crack on the northwest corner.

Honey Maroon Boulder, south face

Honey Maroon Boulder

4. **Honey Maroon Overhang V8** Climb the overhanging west face via a crimpy pull start, then to a small layback and then jug.

5. **Honey Route V3** Climb the crystally face on southwest corner of the boulder.

6. **Moon V2** Climb the left side of the south face using the ground flake for a foothold.

7. **Honeymoon V1** Climb the right side of the south face via good holds.

MOBY DICK ROCK

Continue up the road around the curves eventually heading back to the south. Head south to a point where the road begins to level out. The rock is located off the road to the east, approximately 100 yards across the meadow.

MOBY DICK SOUTH FACE

1. **Moby Dude V1** Climb up the left side of the overhanging shield.

2. **Air Jordan V3** Plant feet and hands firmly below the shield and double-dyno.

3. **Ahab V2** Climb up the right side of the shield via small holds.

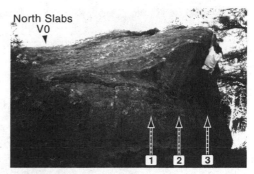

Moby Dick Rock

MOBY DICK NORTH FACE

Several classic V0 slab lines can be done on this north side.

MICKEY MOUSE MEADOW (WEST)

The boulders found in these meadows are quite amazing, offering incredible face climbing on vertical to slightly overhanging walls.

Directions: You can access these boulders by continuing up the road from the Honey Maroon Boulder. However, instead of heading back to the south from the curves, you continue to the north up and through the roadcut toward the old quarries (see Map). The other way, which is usually my choice, is to park at the Fowler Trailhead in the back of Eldorado Canyon and take the trail up to the east, past the Bastille, through the ridge that cuts around to the south. You must then take a right heading up the dirt road toward the old quarries, up to the Mickey Mouse Wall Trail trailhead (see Map). The first boulder, the Golden Nugget, is located a few feet up the Mickey Mouse Trail just as you leave the dirt road and come onto the thin pathway. The Deck Block is located by taking the first small trail leading from the dirt road, a gully trail just before the main Mickey Mouse Wall Trail (See Map). Adam's Spire is found a ways up the Mickey Mouse Wall Trail, across the meadow where the trail levels out just before it turns steeply uphill heading to the wall.

THE GOLDEN NUGGET

This excellent gem of a boulder is located just beside the beginning of the Mickey Mouse Wall Trail, shortly after leaving the dirt road. Look to the right (southeast) side of the boulder, which sits very close to the trail, for many V0 slabs. The west and north sides offer the steep problems.

1. **Ripples V3** Start on the far-left side of the north face and traverse to the right finishing up the bulge.
2. **Nipples V2** Climb out the center of the bulging north face wall.

Kevin Klee ascends the Pebble Hop *(V1) on the Golden Nugget.*

The Golden Nugget

3. **The Bump V3** Climb the right side of the north face via crystal pinching.

4. **The Nugget V4 (B1)** Climb up the northwest corner utilizing small edges.

5. **Golden One V3** Climb the first line of small crystals right of *The Nugget*.

6. **Pebble Hop V1** Climb up the center of the west face via big pebbles.

7. **Gold Digger V4** A thin single crystal is utilized to gain the top.

8. **Golden Girl V2** From the good pocket, reach up to the edges and pebbles.

9. **Fools Gold V1** Climb the crystals and edges on right side of the west face.

10. **She Like Gold V1** Climb the far-right side of the west face.

11. **Necklace V1** Climb the vertical slab on the far-right side of the west face.

12. **Golden Nugget Traverse V12** From the far-right side of the west face, traverse to the left, finishing on the north face.

THE DECK BLOCK

This block is located uphill to the north of the Golden Nugget. Hike up the trail for a short ways then head off into a gully on the north (right) side of the meadow. Follow the southern ridge of the gully until you reach this block. It is somewhat hidden in the trees below a semi-quarried slope. Crash pad is recommended.

1. **Hands on Deck V3** Climb up the far-left side of the west face.

2. **Center Route V0** Climb up the center of the west face via good finger buckets.

3. **Off Center V1** Exit out to the right from the center face.

The Deck Block

4. High Five V4 Climb the overhanging wall via small edges to the bucket top.

5. Deckadance V3 Climb the face right of *High Five*.

ADAM'S SPIRE

This spire-shaped rock is found by heading up to the Mickey Mouse Wall Trail from the Gold Nugget until the trail levels out in a nice meadow with small boulders. The spire is just before the trees, up to the west across the meadow.

1. Adam's Face V0 Climb up the south face, left of the crack.

2. Eastern Project V0 Climb up the middle of the east face.

Adam's Spire

ROUTES BY GRADE INDEX

Features and crags are listed in capitals.
Page numbers in *italics* refer to photographs.

5.12

V?

V0

ROUTES BY NAME INDEX

Features and crags are listed in capitals.
Page numbers in *italics* refer to photographs.

ABOUT THE AUTHOR

Boulder, Colorado resident Bob Horan has climbed for over 30 years. As a teenager he climbed the Grand and Middle Tetons in Wyoming, and El Capitan and Half Dome in Yosemite Valley. He has established hundreds of new routes and boulder problems in the Boulder area, pushing standards with such climbs as the first free ascent of the Rainbow Wall (Eldorado Canyon's first 5.13) as well as Beware the Future (5.14) in the Flatirons. He has also dabbled in competition climbing, placing second in the Masters category at the first annual Horsetooth Hang, third in the Men's Elite division at the first National Climbing Competition in Washington, D.C., and second in the Men's Speed Climbing at the first Continental Climbing Championships. Horan has published numerous photographs and articles in various climbing magazines, and authored five books. His interests in painting and drawing have allowed him to recapture a variety of unique climbing experiences throughout his life. At the University of Colorado in Boulder he graduated magna cum laude in psychology and completed an honors thesis in behavioral neuroscience. He has children who now enjoy bouldering with their dad.

ACCESS: It's every climber's concern

The Access Fund, a national, non-profit climbers' organization, works to keep climbing areas open and to conserve the climbing environment. Need help with closures? land acquisition? legal or land management issues? funding for trails and other projects? starting a local climbers' group? CALL US!

Climbers can help preserve access by being committed to leaving the environment in its natural state. Here are some simple guidelines:

• **STRIVE FOR ZERO IMPACT** especially in environmentally sensitive areas like caves. Chalk can be a significant impact on dark and porous rock—don't use it around historic rock art. Pick up litter, and leave trees and plants intact.

• **DISPOSE OF HUMAN WASTE PROPERLY** Use toilets whenever possible. If toilets are not available, dig a "cat hole" at least six inches deep and 200 feet from any water, trails, campsites, or the base of climbs. *Always pack out toilet paper.* On big wall routes, use a "poop tube" and carry waste up and off with you (the old "bag toss" is now illegal in many areas).

• **USE EXISTING TRAILS** Cutting switchbacks causes erosion. When walking off-trail, tread lightly, especially in the desert where cryptogamic soils (usually a dark crust) take thousands of years to form and are easily damaged. Be aware that "rim ecologies" (the clifftop) are often highly sensitive to disturbance.

• **BE DISCREET WITH FIXED ANCHORS** *Bolts are controversial and are not a convenience*—don't place 'em unless they are *really* necessary. Camouflage all anchors. Remove unsightly slings from rappel stations (better to use steel chain or welded cold shuts). Bolts sometimes can be used pro-actively to protect fragile resources—consult with your local land manager.

• **RESPECT THE RULES** and speak up when other climbers don't. Expect restrictions in designated wilderness areas, rock art sites, caves, and to protect wildlife, especially nesting birds of prey. *Power drills are illegal in wilderness and all national parks.*

• **PARK AND CAMP IN DESIGNATED AREAS** Some climbing areas require a permit for overnight camping.

• **MAINTAIN A LOW PROFILE** Leave the boom box and day-glo clothing at home—the less climbers are heard and seen, the better.

• **RESPECT PRIVATE PROPERTY** Be courteous to land owners. Don't climb where you're not wanted.

• **JOIN THE ACCESS FUND!** To become a member, make a tax-deductible donation of $25 or more.

The Access Fund

Preserving America's Diverse Climbing Resources
PO Box 17010 Boulder, CO 80308
303.545.6772 • www.accessfund.org